PACKRAFTING

PACKRAFTING

EXPLORING THE WILDERNESS
BY PORTABLE BOAT

MOLLY ABSOLON

GUILFORD, CONNECTICUT
HELENA, MONTANA

FALCONGUIDES®

An imprint of Globe Pequot
Falcon and FalconGuides are registered trademarks and Make Adventure Your Story is a
trademark of Rowman & Littlefield.

Distributed by NATIONAL BOOK NETWORK

Copyright © 2017 Rowman & Littlefield
Photos by Moe Witschard, except where noted

All rights reserved. No part of this book may be reproduced in any form or by any electronic or
mechanical means, including information storage and retrieval systems, without written permission
from the publisher, except by a reviewer who may quote passages in a review.

British Library Cataloguing in Publication Information available

Library of Congress Cataloging-in-Publication Data available

ISBN 978-1-4930-2747-7 (paperback)
ISBN 978-1-4930-2748-4 (e-book)

Printed in the United States of America

♾™ The paper used in this publication meets the minimum requirements of American National
Standard for Information Sciences—Permanence of Paper for Printed Library Materials, ANSI/
NISO Z39.48-1992.

CONTENTS

ACKNOWLEDGMENTS

I WOULD LIKE TO THANK ALL THOSE WHO PROVIDED GUIDANCE, EXPERtise, ideas, and corrections for this project. Your help ensures that this book reflects the most up-to-date packrafting techniques and equipment. You've also motivated me with new ideas about where to go and what to do with my packraft—ideas I hope I've conveyed in this book to inspire others. Special thanks to Emily McGinty, Forrest McCarthy, and Luc Mehl for reading the text and giving me feedback. Thanks to Thor Tingey and Alpacka Rafts for launching the sport of packrafting and for the use of the historical images in this book. Thanks to Moe Witschard for his beautiful images as well as his input on the text. Moe's photos really make this book—without them it's just another instruction manual; with them it's an aspirational guide to packrafting adventure. Moe's wife, Marlena Renwyck, deserves a shout-out for being his patient model in many of the photos. I look forward to packrafting adventures with the two of you in the future. Finally, thanks to Don and Sarah Carpenter, Julie Mueller and Don Sharaf, Emily Tepe and Dirk Kramer, and Molly and Andy Tyson for paddling with me. You've all informed this book by being part of my own packrafting path.

And, of course, thanks to my husband, Allen O'Bannon. Allen is my adventure partner and the first to read everything I write. He introduced me to packrafting and river travel, so without him, this book would have never happened.

INTRODUCTION

I LOVE BACKPACKING, BUT "FUN" ISN'T THE WORD I USUALLY USE TO describe the experience—at least not when I have been hiking for miles and miles with a load on my back. Nonetheless, I've explored some incredible country using only my feet and been perfectly content . . . that is, until I discovered packrafting.

I remember floating down the South Fork of the Flathead River in the Bob Marshall Wilderness on my first extended packrafting trip and passing a group of hikers walking along the riverbank. We waved and drifted by, quickly leaving them behind as the current carried us. At that

Packrafting can take you places you might never experience on foot. Here boaters float the Tara River in Montenegro.

Hikers head downstream along Alaska's Jago River with their packrafts, looking for water deep enough to paddle.

moment I knew if there was a floatable river on my next backpacking adventure, I was bringing my packraft. Why walk when you can float and enjoy the scenery?

Don't get me wrong; I love hiking. I love scrambling up peaks and walking through alpine meadows dotted with flowers. I love the smell and hushed darkness you experience hiking through old-growth forest. But I also love the different way you experience the wilderness while floating down a river. Rivers give you a totally new perspective on the world around you. The skills you need are nothing like those you use to move across the land. Your senses are alert to the way the current travels and the sound the water makes as it flows over rocks or piles up in a rapid. Your body awareness shifts from your feet and legs to your upper body as you twist and turn to move your paddle blade through the water. You experience moments of nervous anticipation above rapids and ecstatic joy at the bottom. And you often float past wildlife—deer, moose, otters, and waterfowl—as you travel downstream.

You can use your packraft to access remote wilderness rivers or to boat urban waterways like the Vrbas River in Bosnia.

For me, and many others, there is something special about river life that brings us back year after year to experience its magic. The fact that with a packraft you can combine that magic with the magic of hiking adds to the power of these trips. You feel more connected to the natural world when you get to be on both land and water during your journey.

Not that packrafting is stress and danger free. It can be cold, wet, and uncomfortable in a packraft when the weather is bad and the water temperature frigid. Big rapids can be scary and river hazards dangerous. But life is not risk free, and I'd hate to give up the joys packrafting brings me because of my fears of what could happen if things went wrong.

WHAT IS A PACKRAFT?

Packrafts are tough, sturdy, forgiving crafts that you can carry in a backpack, on a bike, or in your airplane carry-on bag. With all the necessary equipment—paddle, lifejacket or personal flotation device (PFD), helmet, and so forth—a packraft outfit typically adds about 10 to 15 pounds to your backpacking load. It's not insignificant, but it's definitely manageable, and the doors the equipment opens up for you are huge. With a raft in your backpack, you can opt to hike or boat. You can run a whitewater river or float across a lake. You can hike over a pass, trek down to a river, inflate your boat, and head downstream. Depending on your skills, goals, and imagination, your raft gives you freedom to travel through wild places in ways you never have before.

A friend first introduced me to these little inflatable rafts a few years back. My initial experience was bumping down a roadside Class II whitewater run close to home. And I was hooked. The boats are funny and fun, and they totally changed my relationship to wildlands and whitewater. I'd been in a hard-shell kayak a few times and mostly gotten scared. Packrafts let me run rapids without that fear.

Once bitten, I wasn't just looking for cool places to hike when I perused topographic maps planning my summer adventures, I was also looking for cool places to hike to cool rivers to run. It felt as though the packraft had opened up a whole new world for me to explore.

A packraft setup adds about 15 pounds to your backpacking load but allows you to explore on both land and water. Here two packrafters head toward Shot Canyon in Utah's Canyonlands National Park.

The North Fork of the Virgin River in Utah is only runnable in certain wet years, but it's worth the wait.

Packrafting means something different to almost everyone who tries the sport. For some it's about completing epic trips by foot and boat across huge expanses of territory; for others it's about paddling down a flatwater river in their neighborhood. What you do with your raft is up to you, but first you need to gain a few skills.

This book is designed to introduce beginners to the sport of pack-rafting. We will discuss equipment, skills, repair, reading water, and safety, plus give you some tips on trip planning, basic rescue, and packing for your trip. It's enough information to get you started, but to really learn the sport, find a mentor with more experience who can guide you. You can also find video tutorials on specific skills online to help you refine your technique.

Basic packrafting skills come quickly to most people, but that very ease has the potential to get you into trouble. Water is hazardous—moving water even more so. Just because you find you can maneuver your boat on your first venture out, don't underestimate the years of training that go into making a skilled boater—be humble.

To make packrafting as enjoyable and safe as possible, remember to start slowly, go with someone who knows more than you, pick your objectives carefully and conservatively, and never be afraid to get out and walk when you don't like what you see downstream. If you keep these basic rules in mind, you should be able to steer clear of avoidable danger and will have the pleasure of experiencing our wildlands in a new, fun, and exciting way.

CHAPTER ONE

PACKRAFTING HISTORY

BOATS HAVE ALWAYS BEEN USED FOR TRAVEL, AND MOST EXPLORERS followed river corridors when they ventured into the unknown. Big boats were unwieldy to portage, however. To get around this, early travelers in the western United States and Alaska copied the native inhabitants and created small, lightweight boats out of animal hides and willow frames. These boats could be dismantled, carried to a river, reassembled onshore, and then used to float downstream—the archetypal packraft.

Despite these early origins, the sport of packrafting itself is relatively new. Coloradan Dick Griffith has been credited with the earliest inspiration. With his wife, Isabelle, Dick used an Air Force survival raft to make the first descent of the Urique River in Mexico's Copper Canyon in 1952. While their expedition was a success, it did not result in a packraft revolution. It wasn't until the 1970s, when Australian boaters began using what they called "rubber duckies" to run wilderness rivers, that the sport of river running in personal inflatable boats got a little more traction in that part of the world.

In the United States, the idea of using portable inflatable rafts had yet to take root, however. A few people were carrying rafts and inner tubes into the wilderness to access rivers and lakes, but their influence was limited. In the North Cascades, Don, Walt, and Brian Curtis started using the same surplus raft the Griffiths used in Mexico twenty-some years before to fish alpine lakes deep in the mountains. They ended up creating their own 20-ounce version of the raft, which they sold to

The earliest Alpacka packrafts were shaped like miniature whitewater rafts but made from lighter material so they could be packed up and carried in a backpack. The yellow boat in this photo is a first-generation Alpacka Raft sold in 2002. The green craft is a second-generation boat. ALPACKA RAFT

backcountry anglers for years. But the Curtis raft was not rugged enough for river travel and so remained limited in its scope.

Some hard-core adventurers were willing to drag hard-shell kayaks deep into the mountains far from roads to run whitewater rivers. But it took a hardy soul to commit to that effort. The boats were too heavy and awkward for most people to venture very far afield with them, especially when there were plenty of roadside rivers to run. So despite the fact that there are miles and miles of wilderness rivers that can be accessed by foot, for most of the 1970s and 1980s, boaters remained boaters, driving to their put-ins and takeouts, and backpackers remained backpackers, walking past the flowing streams that ran through the mountains where they traveled.

Dick Griffith returned to the scene in 1982 at the annual Alaska's Wilderness Classic. He was 55 at the time and the old man among the

In Alaska, adventurers jumped on the packraft bandwagon and began using the lightweight, portable rafts to explore the state's remote wilderness. This photo is from a 2004 trip on the Aniakchak River—a classic packraft adventure that includes 10 miles of hiking and a 20-mile float to the sea. Alpacka Raft cofounder Thor Tingey used the Aniakchak in 2001 as a testing ground for the original Alpacka Raft. ALPACKA RAFT

race competitors. As the story goes, when the racers came to a deep glacial river crossing, Griffith, who was trailing behind, caught up to the leaders, pulled a raft out of his pack, inflated it, and floated across, leaving behind his competitors who were trying to steel themselves for a long, icy swim. As Roman Dial reports in his book *Packrafting!*, Griffith told his younger compatriots, "You may be fast, but you young guys eat too much and don't know nothin'. Old age and treachery conquer youth and skill any day."

Griffith's use of a raft transformed the Wilderness Classic. After his coup, racers followed his lead and began to carry rafts to navigate the rivers on the course, launching the sport of packrafting once and for all.

The main packraft manufacturer at that time was Sherpa, a company better known for its snowshoes. Sherpa marketed its packrafts for hunting and fishing, but Alaskan wilderness travelers quickly saw more potential for the boats and began using them during their trips through the state's remote mountain ranges and down its wild rivers. Other rafts—like the one designed by the Curtises—were on the market too, but boaters found that most of Sherpa's competitors did not stand up to the punishment of bumping along rocky rivers, and packrafters quickly deemed the Sherpa alternatives to be too fragile or too small for their purposes. In the early 1990s Sherpa stopped manufacturing its rafts, leaving their users with no choice but to baby along the ones that were still in circulation if they wanted to continue expeditioning in a packraft.

Sherpa packrafts were mainly confined to Alaska. But the Alaskans weren't the only ones playing around in boats. In southern Utah and the Grand Canyon, a few "desert rats" began using cheap pool toys and inflatable kayaks to navigate canyon pools and rivers. Though not designed for these types of adventures, the equipment sufficed and helped the explorers poke into places hard to access by foot. One of those desert rats, Forrest McCarthy, said those experiences whetted his appetite and inspired him to look for hardier options to float rivers near his home in Jackson, Wyoming.

The revolution that really opened up the sport beyond a few hardcore diehards in Alaska took place in the late 1990s, after Alaskan adventurer Thor Tingey and his friends made a couple of long wilderness expeditions that included descents of several cold, glacial rivers. They returned from their adventures complaining about their boats being uncomfortable, wet, unresponsive, and low performing. Tingey and his friends called them "shiver boats," and rather than go out and be miserable again, they turned to Thor's mother, Sheri, to create a better option.

Sheri Tingey had built a reputation for herself as a creative designer and manufacturer of outdoor gear. After talking to her son and others, she came up with a sporty personal raft called "Tingey's Dingy." Tingey played with her design over the next few years, until by the early 2000s she'd perfected the first Alpacka Raft, the original packraft that changed the sport forever.

Alaska continued to be the epicenter of packrafting exploration in the United States in those early years, with Roman Dial being one of

Alpacka Raft was the first company to begin developing the modern packraft. During the evolution of its packrafts, the company experimented with design. Here Alpacka Raft cofounder Sheri Tingey tests an early spray skirt prototype that stretched over the entire boat. The skirts kept water out but were so big they created a hazard during a swim. Alpacka started attaching spray decks to the top tubes in 2004. ALPACKA RAFT

its most prolific adventurers. In the Lower 48, Jackson Hole residents Forrest McCarthy and Tom Turiano—both of whom had played with inflatable crafts to float rivers in the desert—were among the earliest adopters of Alpacka's packrafts, using them in the Absaroka Mountains of Wyoming for their first adventures. Since then the sport of packrafting has continued to grow steadily, with the gear evolving rapidly to accommodate changing demands.

McCarthy equates packrafting's current state to the state of the ski industry in the early 2000s, when fat, shaped skis first came onto the market and revolutionized the sport. There are now a number of companies making packrafts, including AIRE, Kokopelli, and Feathercraft, as well as Alpacka. Raft designs range from pure whitewater boats to

As Alpacka perfected its design, people began using their packrafts to get deep into the wilderness. Here packrafters drag their boats through shallow water on one of the first packraft descents of the Aniakchak River, in 2004. ALPACKA RAFT

The forgiving nature of packrafts quickly gave boaters confidence to test them out in whitewater. Here Alpacka Raft cofounder Thor Tingey runs the "Gates" rapids of the Aniakchak River in 2003 using one of the first renditions of a fixed spray skirt. ALPACKA RAFT

extremely lightweight rafts designed for crossing flatwater. You can get self-bailing packrafts and packrafts that zip open to allow storage in the tubes. People are using their packrafts to descend Class IV whitewater, drop waterfalls, and complete huge traverses around the globe. They are also using packrafts to play in water close to home.

As the water rat says in Kenneth Grahame's book *Wind in the Willows*, "Believe me, my young friend, there is nothing—absolutely nothing—half so much worth doing as simply messing about in boats."

Packrafts are the perfect boat to mess about in. It's time to jump in one to see what all the hype is about.

CHAPTER TWO

PACKRAFTING EQUIPMENT

PACKRAFTING'S ESSENTIAL EQUIPMENT IS PRETTY SIMPLE. YOU NEED A raft, a way to inflate your raft, a paddle, and a lifejacket. The other items you need will be dictated by the nature of your trip. If you just want to cross flatwater in your boat, you don't need much more. If you plan to descend a whitewater river, you need to think about helmets, dry suits, safety equipment, and more. The days of a one-size-fits-all packraft are gone. Nowadays packraft manufacturers are creating specialized boats for different purposes, so it's important that you understand your needs before you start shopping.

To help you figure out what to buy, start by determining your goals and budget. You can easily spend several thousand dollars on gear that is unnecessary if your goal is to simply float across pools in a canyon. On the other hand, if you are planning to tackle serious whitewater, you need to have a boat built to withstand those rigors—and that costs money. The cheapest packrafts cost less than $500; the more specialized performance boats can set you back a couple of thousand.

Choosing Your Gear

1. Flatwater or whitewater?
2. Backcountry wilderness trips or sidecountry day trips?
3. Cold water or warm water?
4. Class III or below? Class III or harder?
5. How much can you spend?

Packrafting equipment needs are determined by the nature of the river you plan to run. For whitewater day trips close to the road, a packraft, PFD, helmet, paddle, throw rope, and appropriate clothing are essential.

Your equipment needs are dictated by your destination and budget. For flatwater boating, you can go with lighter gear.

THE RAFT

Forrest McCarthy divides the different style of packrafts on the market into three categories: ultralight flatwater boats, lightweight wilderness whitewater boats, and mid-weight sidecountry whitewater boats. The price, performance, and weight go up with each category shift.

Flatwater Packrafts

The lightest flatwater packrafts weigh as little as 1.5 pounds, making them an ideal tool for backpackers who want to float across lakes, pools, or slow-moving rivers.

The lightest brand currently on the market is made by Supai Adventure Gear and retails for roughly $270. Supai's raft packs down to the size of a 1-liter bottle. Other brands—Flyweight Design's FlytePacker, NRS's packraft, and the Alpacka Scout, for example—are designed to serve the same function as the Supai, but none come close to it in terms of light weight, low cost, and performance. These boats should not be used for any kind of rocky-river travel. To make them light, the materials used are less durable and cannot withstand the bouncing and bumping off boulders that whitewater requires. If you think you are going to be running rivers, you'll want a beefier packraft that costs and weighs a little more.

Lightweight Wilderness Packrafts

The rafts in this category epitomize the essence of packrafting, at least in its original form. They are rugged enough to be used in Class III

When you do not intend to run whitewater, lightweight packrafts like the Supai shown here are great for getting across a river or pool without having to swim.

Alpacka's earliest lightweight wilderness packrafts were oval shaped, like miniature whitewater rafts. Now most models have pointy ends for more bow-stern stability.

whitewater (though people have run harder rivers in them); they are light enough to be carried on your back along with the rest of your camping gear; and they are small enough to fit into a backpack.

Alpacka was the original leader in this category. The company still manufactures durable, reliable boats, but it has some competition now. Feathercraft, AIRE, and Kokopelli are also making lightweight wilderness packrafts that offer variations on Alpacka's original design and a wider range of price points for people with limited budgets. Kokopelli's rafts sell for less than $1,000, making them one of the more economical packrafts available. Alpacka makes the lightest packraft in this category. Its Alpaca model weighs 5.5 pounds but fits only small people, so it has limited appeal. AIRE's BAKraft is moving closer to a classic inflatable kayak in its shape and design, but it still weighs less than 8 pounds with the inflation bag included.

Each brand has its proponents, whose allegiance to a particular boat is often determined by cost, performance, and durability. You can find reviews for different models online.

More and more companies have begun making packrafts as the sport takes off. This paddler is in a Kokopelli packraft on the Gros Ventre River in Wyoming.

Sidecountry Mid-weight Whitewater Boats

A growing number of people are opting to use packrafts to make side-country runs. The term "sidecountry" is used to describe areas that are easily accessible for day trips and often rely on car or bike shuttles rather than hiking. Because you don't have to carry the boat on your back for miles and miles, you can afford to have a heavier packraft designed specifically for whitewater. These boats include Alpacka's Alpackalypse and Feathercraft's Baylee 2.

The Alpackalypse has internal rigging—knee cups and a foot brace—that puts boaters in a powerful paddling position and makes it easier to roll the raft in the event of a capsize. The Alpackalypse also has a spray skirt that is attached to a rigid coaming on the raft made from two aluminum poles. The spray skirt ups the boat's performance in big water by preventing waves from pouring into the raft and keeping the boater in position for rolling. It also makes the raft heavier (as much as 5 pounds more than a bare-bones packraft) and harder

Self-bailing versus Spray Deck

The biggest packraft innovation in the past few years has been the introduction of self-bailing floors. Now you have a choice of using a self-bailing boat or sticking with a more-traditional spray deck.

Self-bailing floors allow boaters to go without a spray deck or skirt, making it easy to get into and out of the boat in the event of a capsize.

to get into and out of. These rafts are great for boaters looking for a whitewater craft to descend challenging rapids. The rafts are packable, making them a more portable option than a typical inflatable or hard-shell kayak, but they weigh as much as 12 pounds (the Alpackalypse with accessories) and take up a lot more room in your backpack, so they aren't great for multiday expeditions. For the average wilderness packrafter heading for Class III water, these boats are overkill, and the weight and cost (the Alpackalypse retails for roughly $2,000) are unnecessary.

Pros of self-bailing boats:

- Easy to get into and out of the boat quickly.
- Inflated floor creates a more rigid boat, which makes the boat more responsive, agile, and faster.
- Rigidity allows boats to punch through holes and waves.
- Self-bailers surf better.
- Higher seat position gives paddler better vision, better stroke placement, an increased ability to edge, and greater control.
- Inflated floor protects paddler's butt and feet from impacts with rocks.
- Paddlers do not need to go ashore to empty their raft in the event of a swamp.
- Depending on the model and style of inflatable floor, self-bailers track better than many non-self-bailing packrafts.

Pros of spray deck (or cons of a self-bailer):

- Spray deck makes boats warmer and drier, especially important in glacial rivers or cold environments.
- Boats tend to be slightly lighter than those with self-bailing floors.
- Lower seating position creates better stability.

Cons of spray deck:

- Can be hard to get spray deck on and closed properly, especially on some older model boats.

Packraft Accessories

Thigh straps: Most basic packrafts do not come with thigh straps, but they are easy to add should you decide you want to up the performance of your boat. Thigh straps enable you to get your boat on edge and make your raft more responsive because you can use your legs and hips to maneuver rather than solely relying on your paddle for control. You can buy padded, adjustable thigh straps for a precise fit, but padded straps do add weight. If you want to go light, you can make your own straps out of webbing and plastic buckles. These do-it-yourself straps work fine

Spray Skirt versus Cruiser Deck

With a non-self-bailing Alpacka raft, you can choose between a spray skirt that is fully closed in or a cruiser deck that just closes with Velcro. Spray skirt setups include a deck on the raft that uses rigid stays to create a lip or coaming for the skirt to hook over and cinch tightly around the paddler's waist. This makes them more watertight and better for rolling, surfing, and performance, but it also makes them heavier and harder to get into and out of. Cruiser decks are lighter, but they don't keep all the water out and can be annoying to close. Many people dislike cruiser decks because of these issues and opt for spray skirts.

Cruiser Deck

Spray Deck

in moderate water and save you a few ounces in the overall weight of your gear.

If you are coming into packrafting with no whitewater kayaking experience, consider practicing wet exits in a pool or flatwater with your thigh straps in place.

See chapter ten for instructions on installing thigh straps in your packraft.

Designed for whitewater, Alpacka's Alpackalypse model weighs and costs more than less-specialized boats.

Thigh Strap Pros and Cons

While there are advantages to thigh straps, there are also disadvantages. One, they add weight and volume if you are carrying your packraft in a backpack. Two, there is a risk of leg entrapment anytime you add straps or lines to a boat. In general, thigh straps probably don't add any value for Class I water, but if you are running rapids—even Class II rapids—thigh straps help you control your packraft. If you are paddling flatwater, save the weight and leave the straps off. In stronger currents, thigh straps will definitely improve the performance of your packraft. If you come from a kayaking background, you'll notice the difference between having straps and not the first time you eddy out.

Once you begin pushing the difficulty of the water you run, thigh straps become critical for control. Even in easier water, they will make your packraft more responsive and allow you to use your body more effectively to maneuver.

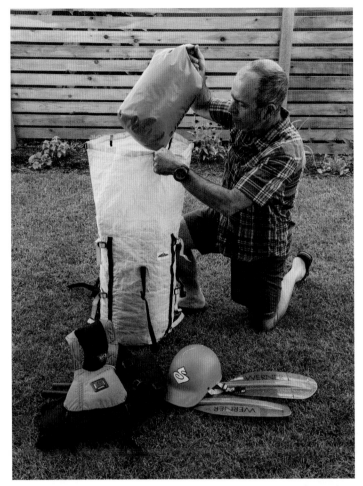

Make sure you waterproof your gear inside your backpack for paddling. The best option is to pack in lightweight dry bags and place the dry bags inside your backpack. You can also find large lightweight dry bags that you can place your backpack inside. In a pinch, lining your pack with garbage bags helps keep things dry.

Cargo: Cargo storage depends on the type of packraft you use. The basic way to carry your gear is to strap a backpack onto the bow of your boat. Alpacka's cruiser decks include tie-downs for your pack, but many people like to reinforce these straps with webbing or accessory cord to secure the backpack in place. You can line your backpack with a garbage bag to keep your clothes dry, but if you plan to do a lot of packrafting, it's worth investing in a lightweight dry bag to ensure your pack is watertight. You can buy Alpacka rafts that include a waterproof zipper in the raft tubes so you can stash your gear inside. This feature allows you to distribute the weight of your gear more evenly around the boat and keeps your bow free of a vision-reducing load, but you need to be careful with the zippers. Keep them clean and handle them gently to ensure they last.

Some Alpacka packrafts come with waterproof zippers, allowing you to store your gear inside the air tubes rather than on top of the bow.

Stern line: Some people like to have a line on their packraft to help them maneuver it when out of the water. If you want a stern line, tie about 4 to 5 feet of accessory cord to the stern tie-down on your boat with a bowline knot. This cord can be used to line your boat along the shore or to tie the boat down in the wind. It is also useful for cinching a deflated raft into a neat package for packing.

A stern line can be used to line your packraft around obstacles, to grab onto in the event of a swim, to tow a swimmer, or to tie up your deflated packraft for transport.

Inflation system: Your packraft will include some kind of inflation bag or pump to force air into the raft. Most companies use a simple nylon bag; others have more elaborate systems. Most rafts take less than 5 minutes to inflate.

Seats: Some packrafts come with an inflatable seat and backrest. The comfort and efficacy of these seats vary. Like a lot of boaters, you may

Most packrafts are inflated with a nylon bag that captures air and allows you to force the air into the tubes.

find that you want to replace the seat that comes with your raft with a higher-quality option for greater comfort and a more efficient paddling position. Feathercraft makes a nice inflatable seat and backrest.

In a self-bailing packraft, paddlers generally sit on the inflated floor, which provides plenty of protection from rocks underneath. You will probably want a backrest, however. Many early adopters of the BAKraft have installed backrests designed for hard-sided kayaks for increased comfort and a better paddling position.

A line along the top of the packraft tubes, either all the way around or along the bow, gives you something to grab onto if you come out of your boat or need to maneuver it around an obstacle. Make sure the line is flush with the surface of the packraft tube to minimize entrapment potential.

Grab line: If you come out of your boat, it can be tricky to get back in without something to grab onto. The tubes feel slippery and big, especially if you are small. Consider creating a grab line by gluing three tie-down patches evenly spaced around the top of the tubes at the bow and stern of your packraft. Run a piece of 3-millimeter accessory cord through the tie-downs at the bow and a second piece through the tie-downs at the stern of the boat. Do not run the cord along the lateral tubes, where it can easily catch on things like your PFD or knife during reentry.

Tie the cord so that it lies flush against the tubes without any slack. Slack creates an entrapment hazard should you fall out of your boat. There is some debate as to whether the grab line should be strung through intermediate tie-downs or tied at each one. The advantage to stringing the line is that cutting it releases the entire cord.

PADDLES

As with your packraft, your paddle choice will be dictated by your goals and budget. You can spend less than $100 or more than $400 on a paddle; depending on what you plan to do with it, either option is valid.

For ultralight packrafting, you can buy individual carbon blades that can be attached to a trekking pole to paddle across short sections of flatwater. Obviously this option has its limitations—imagine paddling any distance with your hands gripped around a skinny ski pole—but at a mere 6 ounces and around $40, it's hard to get much lighter or cheaper unless you forgo a paddle altogether and use your hands to propel your boat.

At the other end of the spectrum, Werner makes a 25-ounce, four-section carbon sea-kayaking paddle that retails for $400. The paddle is durable, light, packable, and high performing, making it ideal for serious wilderness packrafters.

In between these options, you can find paddles from a number of different companies. To help you narrow your choices, here are a few key factors to consider:

- **Materials:** Carbon paddles are lighter than fiberglass paddles, but they are also pricier and tend to be a bit more fragile.

- **Breakdown:** The best wilderness paddles break down into at least two (better yet, four) pieces. Two-piece paddles can be slid under the compression straps on the outside of your backpack for transporting, but beware of low-hanging tree limbs when you are hiking. The paddle shafts tend to stick up above your head high enough to catch on branches. Four-piece paddles get small when you take them apart, making them easier to pack. If you do a lot of roadside paddling, it's worth investing in a one-piece day-trip paddle that will be more durable.

- **Weight:** The lightest paddles that are durable enough for whitewater weigh between 25 and 32 ounces. You can find breakdown paddles that weigh more, but for wilderness expeditioning, you'll want the strongest and lightest paddle you can afford.

- **Cost:** Paddles start at around $100 and go up from there. If you are a beginner paddler who dreams only of running Class III riv-

Breakdown paddles make hiking with your paddle easier. You can find paddles that break down into two or four pieces. Four-piece breakdowns are the easiest to pack.

ers and below, you don't need a top-of-the-line paddle. Be honest with yourself.

- **Length:** Choosing a paddle length for your packraft takes some experimentation and, again, will be dictated in part by the type of water you plan to paddle. For flatwater, a paddle between 197 and 205 centimeters is nice. You can be a bit lazier with a long paddle, but if you want power and the ability to make quick strokes, it's better to go with a paddle between 193 and 197 centimeters.

  Long paddles are best suited for low-angle strokes. For whitewater you want to make high-angle strokes, have the ability to change position quickly, and be able to brace with power, all of which are easier to do with a shorter paddle.

PERSONAL FLOTATION DEVICES (PFDS)

Personal flotation devices (PFDs) or lifejackets are an essential piece of packrafting gear, but choosing one can be tricky. Again, your decision

US Coast Guard Lifejacket Classifications

- **Type I** lifejackets have a minimum of 22 pounds of flotation and are designed for extended survival in rough water far from shore.
- **Type II** lifejackets are the classic lifejacket. They have a minimum of 15.5 pounds of flotation and are intended to be used on inland waterways where rescue is usually quick. Most Type II PFDs are designed to turn an unconscious person face-up. They are the ones with the flap behind the head and are often used by commercial whitewater rafters for their clients.
- **Type III** lifejackets are generally the most comfortable and sleekest. Designed for use during sports like paddling or waterskiing, Type III PFDs provide a minimum of 15.5 pounds of flotation. They will not turn an unconscious person face-up.
- **Type V PFDs/Special-Use Devices** include PFDs that can be inflated to provide up to 22 pounds of flotation. Such devices should only be used for the specific purpose for which they are intended. Read the label before deciding if it is appropriate for your use.

Type V inflatable lifejackets are undoubtedly the lightest, most packable option for packrafters; however, most river run-

should be dictated by your goals and budget. If you plan to boat on flatwater, you can get away with an inflatable Type V life vest like those made by Stormy Seas. If you are going to be running whitewater, you'll want a Type III vest designed for kayaking.

Most adults need at least 12 pounds of flotation to keep their head above water. But for whitewater the recommended minimum is 15.5 pounds. The US Coast Guard rates lifejackets according to their intended use and minimum buoyancy. The more buoyant the vest, the bulkier it will be. For packrafters, that bulkiness can be a significant drawback. You may have the lightest, tightest backpack around, but then you have to figure out where to strap on a big PFD. On the other hand, that big PFD may save your life.

Keep in mind that denser, more muscled bodies need more flotation to stay on the surface, as do nonswimmers. But that flotation doesn't have

For flatwater rivers or lakes, Type V inflatable PFDs (as shown above) are a packable, lightweight option.

ners consider them inappropriate for whitewater. They can rupture and lose all their buoyancy, and to reach their maximum flotation they need to be fully inflated, which can be uncomfortable and make paddling difficult. But if you are in easy water, these jackets are great.

to go to waste. Lifejackets can double as an insulating layer, especially when worn with a windshirt. Or you can use yours as a pillow at night.

For Class III water and above, it is recommended that you opt for a Type III lifejacket designed for kayaking. You can find some inexpensive, low-tech models that work well for packrafting. Or you can opt for a high-end whitewater lifejacket if you plan to spend a lot of time in your boat on harder water.

Look for the following characteristics for the optimal packrafting PFD:

- Pullover vests or vests with a side zip for comfortable paddling.
- Short torso length that doesn't inhibit your body's rotation.
- Big armholes to help avoid restriction and provide comfort during a long day of paddling.

Type III PFDs designed for whitewater kayaking and canoeing are the best option for packrafters. Look for PFDs that allow you to move freely without tons of unnecessary extras that just add weight.

- Simplicity without too many bells and whistles that add weight. It's nice to have a pocket for lip balm, sunscreen, and a knife, as well as a whistle attached to your zipper. Everything else is extra and unnecessary.
- Lightweight and compact PFDs make packing easier.
- Colorful fabric and reflective tape make you more visible.

Rescue Vests

Rescue vests are designed to provide buoyancy and freedom of movement for paddling whitewater as well as to be used for rescues. The main difference between a rescue vest and a Type III PFD is that a rescue vest includes a built-in Quick Release Harness Belt System (QRHS).

A rescue vest is a tool that has limitations and requires training and consistent practice to use safely and effectively. Most pack-rafters do not need a rescue vest. But if you intend to paddle Class IV water and above, you should wear and know how to use one, which means taking a swiftwater rescue course.

HELMETS

American Whitewater's Safety Code says to "wear a solid, correctly fit-ting helmet when upsets are likely. This is essential in kayaks or covered canoes and recommended for open canoeists using thigh straps and raf-ters running steep drops."

You can "upset" your packraft almost anywhere if you aren't paying attention, but when is the risk of a head injury such that you need a helmet?

Most people can keep their head above water in easy rapids—Class I and II. In moderate or Class III it becomes more challenging. Above Class III and you aren't really swimming if you come out of your boat, you are fighting. Fighting to stay on your back with your feet pointing downstream. Fighting to stay away from rocks and out of recirculating eddies. Fighting for air as you come up out of the water on top of a wave, only to be sucked back under. In these conditions, a helmet is imperative.

If you plan to boat flatwater or easy-moving water without thigh straps, you can forgo wearing a helmet. If you plan to jump into rapids Class III and above, bring one. The best helmets for packrafting are hel-mets designed for kayaking or whitewater canoeing. There are a few great multi-sport models on the market, but using a bike or climbing helmet for whitewater is not recommended. It's better than nothing, but not

If you plan to boat Class III whitewater or above, you should wear a helmet. The best packrafting helmets are those designed for whitewater boating. A visor is a nice option.

ideal. Kayaking helmets are made to withstand the multiple impacts you may encounter if you end up upside down in a rapid. For that reason, it's a good idea to go with a helmet made for whitewater boating.

When looking for a helmet, make sure you find one that is light and strong and fits snugly but not so tightly that you end up with a headache after a few hours in your boat. You need a chinstrap that is secured with a quick-release buckle. Remember, the helmet only works if that buckle is closed.

Helmets that come with a short bill on the front are very effective. They not only help keep some sun off your face but can create an air pocket if you end up face-down in the river, such as what happens in a foot-entrapment scenario.

Carbon helmets are lightweight, but they can cost a couple hundred dollars. Plastic or fiberglass helmets may be slightly heavier, but they tend to cost less than $100. Go to a whitewater boating store and try on a few models to see what you like best.

In cold weather it's nice to wear a lightweight wool beanie under your helmet for added warmth. In extreme conditions you can opt for a fuzzy rubber helmet liner for the most insulation.

WHAT TO WEAR IN YOUR BOAT

Packrafting is wet. Even boats with spray decks tend to take on water if you are moving through whitewater, not to mention that there's always the possibility of a swim if you should capsize, so paddlers need to gauge their attire according to the air and water temperature.

Your choices run from a bathing suit and shorts to rain gear to a wet or dry suit. A bathing suit is fine in the middle of summer when the temperatures are high, the water warm, and you are confident you aren't going to get caught out in a thunderstorm. Rain gear works if you are running easy water and your chance of swimming is minimal. For cold water you should wear either a wet or dry suit to be safe and comfortable.

The American Canoeing Association considers cold-water conditions to be any water that is less than 60°F or when the combined air and water temperature is less than 120°F. In these conditions, swimmers rapidly lose their ability to function as they succumb to the cold and become hypothermic.

Unprotected by any kind of insulation, you are subject to the 1-10-1 rule when immersed in cold water. During that first 1 minute in the water, you'll be incapacitated by cold-water shock. The cold receptors in your skin respond to the sudden decrease in temperature by evoking uncontrolled gasping, hyperventilation, increased heart rate, and vasoconstriction. The gasping will pass, so don't panic while you wait for your body to calm down. Panicking increases the chance you will aspirate water.

In cold-water conditions and chilly weather, bundle up so you stay warm and dry. You'll be more comfortable and safer if you are dressed appropriately for the conditions.

Once the initial shock has passed, you have 10 minutes of functional movement before you lose control of your muscles and can no longer swim or pull yourself out of the water. You then have 1 hour before you are likely to lose consciousness from hypothermia—if you don't drown before that. Insulation gives you more time to withstand the cold water's effects on your body, and therefore can save your life.

For cold-water boating, you need to decide between a dry suit and a wet suit. A dry suit is made from waterproof, breathable material like Gore-Tex that is sealed at the wrists and neck by rubber gaskets and with either gaskets at the ankle or waterproof socks to keep moisture out. Underneath the suit, you stay dry and can layer clothing according to the air temperature. Wet suits are made from neoprene, which traps a thin layer of water next to your skin. Your body heats up this water and keeps you warm.

Some boaters opt for a paddling suit or paddling jackets and pants. Paddling suits tend to have neoprene cuffs and neck closures. Some include built-in socks as well. They keep splashing water out, but if you go for a swim, you'll be wet. The advantage to a paddling suit is weight. Dry suits typically weigh about 50 ounces, while a paddling suit will be closer to 30 ounces. Rain gear is even lighter, but again, it won't do you any good if you go for a swim.

Dry Suits

Dry suits are expensive and can be heavy, but if you plan to boat in cold places, they are worth every dollar and ounce, as most of us are more comfortable—and safer—if we are warm and dry.

Next to your boat, your dry suit is going to be your most expensive piece of equipment, with prices ranging from $600 to more than $1,000. If you are investing that kind of money, it's important to make sure you pick a dry suit that is both comfortable and durable.

Dry suits cost almost as much as a packraft, so it's important to take care of them. After a day of paddling, rinse them off and hang them out to dry.

Here are some key things to consider in your purchase:

- **Material:** Dry suits must withstand a lot of wear and tear. Just paddling in your boat causes your suit to rub as you twist and turn with each stroke. Find a dry suit that is durable and that comes with a lifetime warranty. Gore-Tex is the material of choice, but some brands are being made with other materials. If you opt for a different material, read performance reviews online. The downside to beefy, durable materials is that they weigh more. But for cold-water boating, that added weight is probably worth your added comfort and safety. Dry suits should keep you dry. If yours is leaking, you either have a defective suit or there's a hole somewhere.

- **Fit:** Dry suits themselves do not keep you warm; they keep you dry. To be warm inside you need to wear layers of insulating gear. What you wear depends on the air temperature, so you want a suit that is roomy enough to fit multiple layers of clothing to suit conditions and still let you twist and turn to paddle. Many boaters think Kokatat makes the best dry suit on the market, but other brands are catching up. Each of them has a slightly different fit, so you may find that Kokatat is not the best option for you. Try on different models while wearing the layers you anticipate boating in to make sure you are buying a dry suit that matches your physique.

- **Socks:** It's worth investing in a dry suit that comes with built-in socks. The rubber gaskets on dry suits are their weakest link, so if you can minimize the number of gaskets by eliminating them at your ankles, you'll be happier. Plus built-in socks allow you to wear cozy wool socks on your feet, which will keep you warmer. Most packrafters then wear some kind of boating shoe over the dry suit socks.

- **Relief zippers:** Dry suits come in men's and women's models. Both have zippers that allow you to pee and poop without having to remove your entire dry suit. Keep these zippers clean. Dirt causes them to gunk up and malfunction. Don't yank on a

Dry Suit Tip

To help improve your dry suit's durability, wear a thin neoprene sock over the dry suit booties to help protect the fabric and increase the suit's longevity.

stuck zipper. Clean and lube it with some kind of zipper lube like McNett Zip Tech.

Dry Suit Care and Maintenance

Caring for your dry suit will prolong its life. If you are careful, you can keep one around for seven to ten years, which is nice if you've dropped a grand on it. After you finish boating, rinse your dry suit in fresh water and wipe off the gaskets using a sponge or cloth, warm water, and mild soap. Sunscreen can eat away the latex, so it's important to apply sunscreen to your body carefully to avoid contact with your dry suit gaskets and then to wipe the gaskets off after your trip to ensure no sunscreen inadvertently gets left on them. To dry, hang your dry suit out of direct sunlight in a cool spot. For long-term storage, hang the suit in a cool, dry place or pack it loosely in a plastic storage bin. Keep the zippers flat.

Occasionally you may need to restore the water-repelling capacity of your dry suit by applying some kind of waterproofing fabric treatment. Most boaters recommend Nikwax TX.Direct. Spray the treatment over your suit, then apply heat with an iron or a hair dryer to activate the treatment. If you opt to use an iron, be sure to place a cotton cloth between the iron and your dry suit to protect the fabric. You want to warm the material, not melt it.

Gaskets should be treated with 303 Protectant every six weeks during active use; 303 provides sunscreen protection and helps reduce degradation from UV rays. Spray 303 onto the gasket and let dry. Wipe off excess with a clean, dry cloth.

If your dry suit gaskets get torn or damaged, they are relatively easy to replace. You can find instructions online, but the main thing is to use

Aquaseal and a cylindrical object that can hold the new gasket in place while the glue dries. Luc Mehl, who tinkers with his gear a lot, recommends using mason jars for wrist gaskets and a canister for storing food in bear country for the neck.

Putting On Your Dry Suit

It takes a little practice to master getting in and out of your dry suit easily. Before you start, remove all jewelry or watches to avoid snagging on the latex. You may even want to trim your nails. Then step into the legs and pull the suit up to your waist. Cinch the draw cord around your waist

To pull your dry suit neck gasket over your head, stretch it out with both hands and carefully work it down.

to keep the suit from falling down. Work one arm and then the other into the sleeves, taking care as you push your hands through the rubber gaskets. Once your arms are in, stretch the neck gasket open with both hands and carefully work it down over your head.

If this is the first time you've worn your dry suit, pause to see how the neck gasket feels. It should fit snugly without constricting your throat. If you feel like you are choking, the gasket is too tight. To fix that, stretch the gasket around a pot or a bear canister overnight and try to put it on again the next day. If it is still too tight, stretch the gasket overnight a second time. If that doesn't work, you probably will need to trim the gasket to fit

Be careful zipping your dry suit closed. The waterproof zippers on dry suits are the weakest link; keep yours lubed so it runs smoothly, and always pull it in line.

better. Look for rings imprinted on the latex. Trim away the top ring of the gasket using a sharp knife to ensure that you leave no nicks, and then check the fit again. If you need the gasket to be even looser, trim it down to the next ring. Always trim one ring at a time and try on the suit to test the gasket's fit between trims. There's no going back once that latex is gone.

When your head is through the gasket, reach into the suit and smooth out your clothes. After you are zipped in, it's hard to make sure things are in the right place inside the suit. To avoid an uncomfortable fold or twist in your layers, smooth everything out before you close down the suit.

Your last step to getting into your dry suit is to "burp" the excess air by squatting down and pulling open the neck gaiter.

Finally zip up the closure zipper. This zipper usually is on the front. You may need help getting it completely closed. Once you are locked in, squat down and gently pull open your neck gasket to "burp" the suit or release the excess air. Now you are good to go!

To get out of your dry suit, just reverse the process, taking care with your gaskets.

Semi-Dry Suits

As the name implies, these suits keep you semi-dry. Also known as paddling suits, semi-dry suits generally come with a neoprene neck gasket rather than one made from latex. Neoprene is not waterproof and will allow water in if you flip. Semi-dry suits are lighter and cheaper than dry suits and can be a good option for Class II water and below. In more difficult water it's better to go for a dry suit, especially if it's cold.

Wet Suits

For cold-water paddling on extended wilderness expeditions, wet suits tend to be less useful than dry suits.

To stay warm in cold conditions in a wet suit, you need to wear a full-body, long-sleeved neoprene suit combined with a paddling jacket and pants to block out the wind and cut down on convective heat loss. This kind of wet suit typically weighs about the same as a dry suit and takes up a similar amount of space in your pack—more when you include the paddling jacket and pants. Furthermore, wet suits often take longer to dry than a dry suit. You may as well opt for a dry suit if your goals include cold-water paddling. Wet suits are much, much cheaper, however, and, if that is what you have, it's much better than nothing.

Where wet suits really shine is in milder conditions where you would just steam in your juices inside a dry suit. There are a variety of options for wet suits that keep you comfortable in warmer climes, including farmer johns, shortie suits, HydroSkins, and neoprene shirts and shorts. For summer boating these options tend to be lighter, more packable, and cheaper ($100 to $400) than a dry suit.

Like all boating gear, you'll preserve the life of your neoprene if you take care of it. Rinse your wet suit in fresh water at the end of the day and hang it up to dry away from direct sunlight. Once you get home at the end of a trip, wash the suit in warm water with a mild soap to remove body oils and dirt. Rinse and dry the wet suit thoroughly and store it in a cool, dry place away from the sun. If your wet suit or other neoprene product starts to smell funky, you can buy soaps that kill bacteria and fungi.

ACCESSORIES

Neoprene Socks or Booties, Gloves, Mittens, and Pogies

In addition to wet or dry suits, neoprene socks or booties, gloves, mittens, or pogies can help you stay warm in a wet, cold environment.

In a dry suit with built-in socks, neoprene socks or booties are unnecessary. In a paddling suit or wet suit, they help keep your feet warm during the day. Look for socks that fit snugly and can be worn under your hiking shoes. For booties, avoid lots of buckles to help reduce weight and bulk. Most packrafters do not bring booties on wilderness trips because of space and weight concerns in their backpacks.

The choice between gloves, mittens, or pogies depends on your personal preference, the ambient air temperature, and the type of boating you plan to do. In general, gloves are the least warm option and tend to be hard to remove, but they do allow you to use your fingers for tasks that don't require a lot of dexterity. Play boaters or boaters running highly technical water typically opt for gloves because they want to be able to use their fingers without having to stop and remove a mitten.

Pogies offer the most warmth and are the easiest to get out of if you need to use your hands to perform an intricate task. Mittens come next. They are warmer than gloves and faster to remove.

Gloves

- Too-tight gloves will constrict blood flow and make your fingers cold.
- Nylon coverings on the glove's palms add weight and make it hard to grip your paddle.
- Nylon coverings on the back of the hand protect the neoprene from tears but add weight and increase evaporative cooling.

For cold-weather paddling, neoprene gloves can help keep your hands warm and allow you the dexterity to perform intricate tasks.

Mittens

Mittens are warmer than gloves, but you won't be able to do anything that requires dexterity without taking them off. It can be cumbersome to deal with the on-off routine if you anticipate making lots of adjustments.

Pogies

Pogies attach to your paddle, creating a mitt that protects your hand from splashing water and wind, but still allow you to remove your hand easily if you need to use your fingers.

Boating Shoes

For most wilderness packrafting, you'll boat in your hiking shoes. You can find lots of options designed for both the river and the trail on the

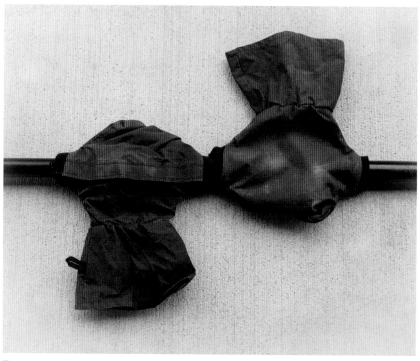

For super cold and wet conditions, pogies are the warmest option for your hands, particularly when worn with neoprene gloves underneath.

market. As you sort through your shoe choices, look for the following features:

- Shoes that are comfortable, supportive, and lightweight. (For most trips, low-top shoes will suffice, but if you anticipate a lot of rough, off-trail hiking and boulders, you might want to wear a lightweight hiking boot for more ankle support.)
- Shoes made from nonabsorbent, quick-drying, durable fabric. (Avoid so-called waterproof shoes. No shoe is waterproof if you submerge it in water. Waterproof coatings tend to just trap water inside.)
- Shoes with sticky rubber soles that provide traction as well as protection and cushioning on the trail.

The ideal packrafting shoe is one you can hike in as well as wear in your boat. Look for lightweight, comfortable, supportive shoes that have a sticky sole for walking over rocks.

- Shoes with a secure lacing system.
- Shoes that are roomy enough to go over dry suit booties and socks or neoprene socks. (You can opt to pull the insoles out of your shoes so you have extra space to fit your shoes over your dry suit and a warm pair of socks.)
- The jury is out on the benefits of mesh shoes for packrafting. Shoes with mesh are lighter and more breathable and dry quicker than shoes without. The mesh also allows water to drain out. The downside is that sand can come in through the mesh, making the shoes uncomfortable.

SAFETY EQUIPMENT

You need to carry some basic rescue equipment if you plan to paddle swiftwater. Remember, carrying safety gear is useless if you don't know how to use it. If you intend to tackle wilderness whitewater in your packraft, take a swiftwater rescue course or practice basic rescue techniques on your own. We will go into more detail on basic rescue later in this book.

Each individual should carry a throw bag, knife, and whistle. Store the whistle where you can get to it quickly, especially if you are in the water. A lot of people like to hang their whistle from the zipper pull of their PFD. Whistles are used to sound the alarm when something goes wrong, such as when a boater flips or gets pinned.

River knives allow you to extract yourself if you get entangled in a rope or pinned in your packraft. Again, the knife has to be handy to be useful. Most river knives are big and bulky and can be attached to the outside of your lifejacket, which is important in an emergency. However, when pack weight is a major concern, consider whether you might be better off carrying a small, multipurpose knife that cuts cheese as well as ropes instead of a heavy, bulky river knife hooked onto your PFD. A smaller knife can be stashed in your PFD pocket. This option is a compromise, because a knife in your pocket is not as accessible as a knife on the outside of your lifejacket. But the reality is that most boaters only use their knives to spread peanut butter on bread during lunch breaks. You should be fine going with a light knife and carrying it in a pocket.

Throw ropes are used to pull swimmers to shore and to retrieve pinned boats. The ropes come stuffed in a nylon sack that has a piece of foam on the bottom so the sack floats. The rope should also float and have a minimum ⅜-inch diameter so it's easy to hold onto. The lightest rope option is polypropylene. Some whitewater boaters prefer Spectra cord for its superior strength. Spectra is slightly heavier and more expensive, but it is strong enough to use it in a 3-to-1 pulley system. It's very unlikely you will ever need to build a 3-to-1 to dislodge a pinned packraft—packrafts can be deflated, which usually reduces the pin—but you may need the mechanical advantage provided by a 3-to-1 to do things like move wood while clearing a section of river or to help rescue a bigger, heavier boat.

Throw ropes typically come in either 55- or 75-foot lengths. The longer ropes are useful for 3-to-1 pulley systems, but for rescuing swimmers and on smaller rivers, you are fine with the shorter length. Not many of us can throw 75 feet with any accuracy. The reality is that you'll need to

There are a wide variety of throw ropes on the market. Look for one that is at least 55 feet long.

get close to reach a swimmer with a throw rope, meaning 55 feet should be just fine.

Choose a throw rope that comes in a roomy stuff sack. You want to be able to get the rope in and out of the bag quickly and easily; if it's a tight fit, you'll get frustrated.

A lot of people clip their throw rope to the side of their packraft. This technique is risky—the cord can come out and get wrapped around obstacles, creating a hazard. The best option is to carry your throw rope on your body. Some ropes come with a waistband so that you can wear it. Or you can stuff the bag down the front of your PFD, although many people don't like the added bulk this creates, and it can make reentering your raft difficult in the event of a flip. Clipping the rope to the packraft with a carabiner is also potentially hazardous. Accidentally throwing the bag with the biner attached is a good way to chip someone's tooth or cause a black eye.

REPAIR KITS

In the wilderness our gear is critical to our safety, and we can't just go to the store for a new part. Backpackers need to carry—and know how to use—a few essential repair items on all wilderness trips. For example, you should have spare parts and cleaning tools for your stove. You probably need a patch kit for your sleeping pad if you have one that inflates, and Tyvek tape always comes in handy for repairing tears in clothing and gear. Repair kits also can include a spare set of batteries for your various electronics. See the complete Group Repair Kit list in appendix D.

Packrafting adds a few more items to the basic repair kit list. Most packrafts are surprisingly tough. It's hard to put a hole in one, but punctures do happen—especially if you encounter a lot of wood on your float. Small holes in the floor are the most common place to see a leak. These holes are easy to fix with a blob of Aquaseal or Seam Grip.

If the tear is bigger or you are in a hurry and can't wait for the Aquaseal to cure, you will need a patch. For emergency repairs, Gear Aid's Tenacious Tape repair patches and tape (mcnett.com/gearaid/max-repair-patch#10800) let you repair holes quickly, and often the patches last indefinitely. Tyvek or Patch-N-Go tape also works well for creating temporary patches. For the most effective use of tape, it's a good idea to carry scissors in your repair kit to round corners and cut pieces.

We'll go into details on basic repair and provide a sample repair kit list in chapter ten.

In chapter eleven we will discuss personal and group equipment needs for a wilderness packrafting expedition.

CHAPTER THREE

GETTING STARTED

ONCE YOU HAVE YOUR EQUIPMENT, IT'S TIME TO GET IT ON THE WATER. To prepare for a day on the river, there are a few things you need to do to get your gear ready.

INFLATING YOUR PACKRAFT

Different brands of packrafts come with different inflation systems, but most rely on some kind of nylon bag rather than a pump to get air into

A paddler has fun in a self-bailing packraft on Montana's Gallatin River.

Author's Tip

Use a small piece of 3-millimeter utility cord to attach the valve cap for your boat to a tie-down. The caps are small and easily lost, which will really ruin your day.

the tubes. The beauty of the airbags is that they are extremely lightweight and low tech, which is just what you want on a wilderness trip.

Most packrafts have a single tube, so you only have to fill that tube to get your boat ready. If you have a self-bailing boat, you'll also need to inflate your floor. Alpacka now makes boats with an internal cargo fly, which allows you to store gear in the rear tubes via a waterproof zipper. The inflation process for these boats has a few extra steps, but you still follow the same basic procedure.

Inflation bags are usually simple rip-stop nylon sacks that are open at one end, with either rigid bars or handles on either side. There will be a nozzle at the closed end.

Step 1: Screw the nozzle into the packraft's air valve. Just make a couple of rotations with the nozzle to make it easier to remove the bag at the end without losing a lot of air in the process.

If you make ten or so counterclockwise twists in the sack just above the nozzle before you start screwing, you'll end up without any twists in your bag when the nozzle is screwed down. If you don't, make sure you untwist the bag before you begin inflating the boat.

Put the valve cap in your pocket; better yet, let it hang from the leash you've made to secure the cap to your boat.

Step 2: Pull the bars or handles apart, opening the bag. Bend over, collapsing the bag, then pull the bag up toward your waist to capture a pocket of air. If there is a breeze, you can just open the bag toward the wind to fill it up. Bring the bars or handles together, grab the bag below them, and pinch it closed. Some people like to make a twist here; others make a quick roll in the fabric. You'll figure out what works best and fastest for you.

Step 3: Press the bag against your legs or body to force the air into the packraft.

Step 4: Repeat Steps 2 and 3 until you cannot get any more air into your boat.

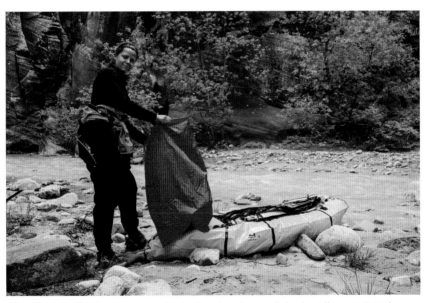

After the inflation bag is screwed into the air valve, pull the handles apart and extend the bag open.

Capture a bagful of air and then twist or pinch the bag closed.

Press the bag against your legs to force air into your packraft.

Step 5: Unscrew the airbag and replace the valve cap.

Step 6: Top off the boat by blowing air into the raft. Alpacka Rafts have a top-off tube with a mouth valve on it. Others brands have a one-way valve on the cap that you can blow air into.

Step 7: Temper your boat. The air you blow into your raft is warm and will contract when it comes into contact with cold river water. To keep the tubes firm, place the raft in the water for a few minutes before you get in to head downriver. Splash the tubes to cool down the air inside.

When you can no longer get air into the raft with your airbag, remove the bag, close the valve, and blow air into the top-off tube until your packraft is firm.

Once the raft starts to feel soft, blow more air into the tube until it feels firm to the touch again. You want your boat to be as rigid as possible for peak performance. In icy water, say a glacial river, you may need to add air to your boat a few times until you get the right pressure in the tubes.

SECURING YOUR SEAT

When the only option for packrafters was Alpacka, the next step in your setup would have been to inflate your seat and backrest. Today different boats come with different setups, and some do not even have a seat.

Depending on your style of boat, once the packraft is inflated, you'll want make sure your seat is inflated.

Packraft seats tend to feel low, especially if you are a small person or come from a whitewater background. Too low a seat makes it hard to paddle effectively. You'll find it challenging to engage your core and get leverage on your paddle strokes if you are deep down in your boat. Plus, a load on the bow of your boat can block your vision if you are too low.

This Alpacka packraft has been modified with a backrest by Jackson Kayak and an aftermarket seat to give the paddler a higher position in the boat as well as provide more comfort.

If you feel too low, you may want to substitute a beefier model for the seat that came with your boat. (Feathercraft makes an inflatable seat and backrest that gets you up higher off the floor of your raft than the seats that come with Alpacka packrafts.) You can also install a second seat to give you a boost—so two Alpacka seats stacked on top of each other. With this method, you can adjust your height by adding or subtracting air.

Finding the perfect height takes a little time in the boat, however; so for your first few adventures, you'll be fine with what came with your packraft.

ATTACHING A LOAD

Traditionally, packrafts were designed to have a backpack or dry bag strapped onto the bow, and for many boats this is still the standard way to carry a load. Older boat designs actually ride better with a load, as the

Many packrafts come with some kind of system for carrying a load, but you may find it's best to rig something beefier to make sure things are held in place securely. This packrafter has used webbing to create tie-down straps on her packraft during a trip on the Kongakut River in Alaska.

weight upfront helps balance out the paddler's weight in the back so you don't pop a wheelie when you hit a big wave.

In his book *Packrafting!* Roman Dial says the optimal bow load in moderate whitewater is around 20 to 35 pounds. That weight keeps the bow down and allows the raft to track better through the water. That said, packrafts spin with very little effort when unloaded, making them highly maneuverable, which can be nice when you need to make quick moves. Furthermore, packraft designs have evolved, and most now feature pointier ends that minimize the risk of popping wheelies.

Your packraft may come with straps for securing your pack in place. Alpacka supplies a tie-down system on its cruiser deck that includes a quick-release buckle for easy access. But that system isn't very beefy, and

A simple way to attach your backpack is to run two webbing straps through the bow tie-downs and across the load. Use a plastic slider to allow easy adjustments.

it can be hard to keep your load from shifting without reinforcement. Many packrafters have opted to create their own tie-down system.

One of the easiest options is to add two 2-foot sections of 3- or 4-millimeter utility cord to the bow tie-downs. You can wrap these cords around your load and tie them off using a quick-release trucker's hitch. Another technique is to use two bungee cords around 18 inches long to secure your load. Or you can use 6-foot webbing straps with plastic buckles.

Before strapping down your pack, make sure it is waterproofed. One way to do this is to pack everything you want to keep dry in a lightweight dry bag inside the pack. In mellow water you can substitute a garbage bag for a dry bag, but garbage bags don't hold up that well during a multiday trip, so if you plan to packraft, it's worth investing in a dry bag. If you intend to do a lot of wilderness packrafting, consider buying a Sea to Summit Big River Dry Bag that you can put your backpack inside. These dry bags have low-profile lash loops along the sides that allow them to be strapped onto your packraft securely. Made from an abrasive-resistant, durable, waterproof material, they stand up to hard use. The benefit of having your dry bag on the outside of your pack is that it protects your backpack. Plus the dry bag doesn't have lots of straps hanging off of it, so you end up with a more streamlined, safer load with fewer lines to entangle you if you go for a swim. Sea to Summit dry bags vary in weight according to size, ranging from 2.5 ounces for a 3-liter bag to 10 ounces for one that holds 65 liters.

Beware of hard items or sharp edges in your pack. Your packraft will bend and fold as it moves through rapids; that movement can cause the pack to rub against your raft, causing wear and tear, or it can push sharp edges through the dry bag, creating a hole. You can avoid this by making sure fuel bottles and other hard items are wrapped up in clothing or your sleeping bag to cushion them. If you have trekking poles, collapse them down to their smallest size and cinch them down on top of your pack.

If your backpack is on the outside, cinch down all the straps on your pack so there are no loops or lines that could ensnare you. Then flip the pack over so the hip belt and shoulder straps face down when you place

Trucker's Hitch

Probably the most useful hitch there is, the trucker's hitch allows you to pull a line super tight and is therefore a great way to secure a load whether it's on a truck, a tent, or your packraft.

1. One end of your line must be tied off to a fixed anchor of some sort. On your packraft this fixed point will be a tie-down loop.
2. Place the other end of the line—or the working end—across your load and feed it through a tie-down on the opposite side from your fixed point. This creates a bend, or change of direction, in the line and allows you to pull it back toward the fixed end.
3. Make a slipknot in the fixed end. Make sure you pull the line from the working-end side through to create your slipknot; otherwise the loop will close down on itself when you cinch down your load.
4. Feed the working end of your line through the slipknot and pull away from the fixed end until the line is tight. Pinch the working end next to the slipknot to hold it in place.
5. Now tie off the hitch with two half hitches. If you want to make it slippery, use a bight in your hitch to create a slipknot.

it on the bow of your boat. That way you don't have a lot of loops and straps exposed on top.

Most of the time, it works best to secure your load perpendicular to the boat's long axis. It seems to balance best in this position, and it's easy to maintain a low profile so that your vision is not impaired.

Sometimes, however, there are advantages to orienting the backpack in line with the raft's long axis. In this case, place the pack so the hip belt is close to the bow of your boat and the top of the pack points toward the rear. Keep the shoulder straps and hip belt facing up. This position works well when you anticipate a lot of portages. It allows you to wear your backpack without removing it from the boat so that

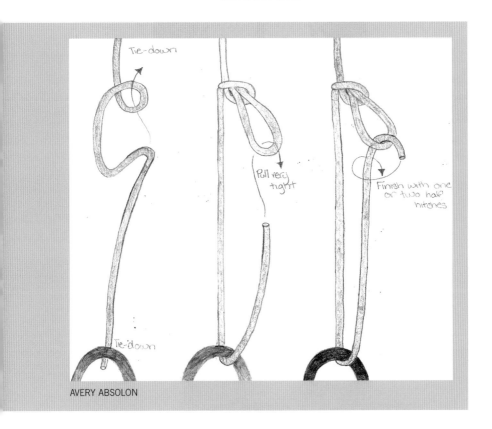

AVERY ABSOLON

you can carry your packraft around an obstacle on your back. ***Beware:*** Leaving the shoulder straps up creates loops that could entrap your foot or other parts of your body if you were to go for a swim. You can free the shoulder straps from the slider near the hip belt so they are loose and do not cause an entrapment hazard or cinch them down tightly to minimize the risk.

Once your pack is positioned on the boat, take the accessory straps, bungee cord, or webbing you've attached to the bow and feed it through your pack's compression straps. Hook the straps on the opposite side and cinch them down tightly. With smaller packs, it works well to cross the straps over the load. Bigger loads usually work best with the straps

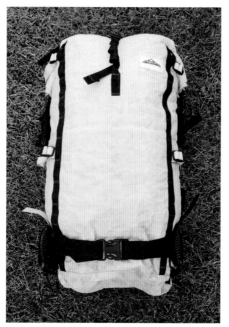

Cinch down all the straps on your backpack to avoid entrapment hazards when you place it on the bow of your packraft.

Packrafters in the Arctic are loaded down for a backcountry adventure.

running parallel to each other. Make sure the pack doesn't shift or move around if you shake it. You want that load to stay in place, whatever happens.

GETTING INTO YOUR BOAT

The best way to get into your boat is to find an eddy with unmoving water. Place your boat in shallow water along the shoreline. Lay your paddle across the bow of your packraft and hold on with your outside or river-side hand. Place the other hand on the packraft tube.

Step into the boat. You can stand on the floor of your packraft, but be careful you are not stepping on sharp rocks or sticks that could poke a hole through it.

To get into your packraft, hold onto your paddle and the opposite tube for balance and step carefully onto the floor. Avoid sharp rocks or sticks beneath your packraft.

Once both feet are in the boat, sit down.

If your boat has a spray deck or spray skirt, attach that now. Make sure you reach behind and pull the deck up and over your lifejacket. You want it as high as possible to keep water out. Spray skirts, on the other hand, are typically worn *under* a PFD and put on before you get in the boat. Once you are seated, attach the spray skirt to the raft's coaming. Self-bailing rafts do not have a spray deck, so once you are seated, you are good to go.

Author's Tip

It can get pretty hot and clammy inside a spray deck if the sun is out and you are paddling flatwater. Spray decks and skirts are designed to keep splashing water out of your raft. If there's no way splashing water is going to come into your craft, you don't have to secure your spray deck. Other situations where you may not want the skirt secured include places where you anticipate lots of getting into and out of your boat (portages or scouting), times when you opt to paddle without a helmet, and tricky conditions where it can be hard to get the skirt on, such as a difficult place to launch.

PACKING UP AT THE END OF THE DAY

After you finish paddling, it's time to put your gear away. You've invested a lot of money in your equipment, and proper care will ensure that it lasts a long time.

To begin, open all the air valves and let the packraft and seat deflate. You can speed things up by gently lying on the tubes to force air out of the packraft.

Once the packraft is fully deflated, place it flat on the ground. Fold the sides in along the vertical axis of the raft so that it is folded in thirds lengthwise. Make sure the air valve is not blocked. Tightly roll the boat toward the exposed valve, forcing any remaining air out of the tubes.

Once the raft is rolled up, close the air valve. Tie the roll securely with a strap or the stern line on your boat.

To make your packraft super flat, unroll it so you can suck any remaining air out through the inflation tube. Then reroll it for packing.

Author's Tip

Sometimes you'll find it's easier to pack your packraft into your backpack folded rather than rolled. You'll still deflate it by rolling, but once all the air is out, unroll the raft. Then fold it into a square package and tie with a strap or the boat's stern line.

CLEAN AND DRY

When you get home from your trip, you need to clean and dry your packraft before storing it. Pull the packraft out of your backpack and inflate it. It doesn't have to be super tight, but inflating it speeds up drying in nooks and crannies.

Waterborne invasive species threaten the biodiversity and health of our watersheds. You can avoid accidentally spreading these pests by rinsing all your boating gear in fresh water (make sure you hose out under your boat tubes and in cracks and crevasses to remove all hitchhikers) and

When you get home from a packrafting trip, rinse your boat out thoroughly to ensure you aren't accidentally transporting waterborne invasive species. Clean equipment will also last longer.

drying it thoroughly for a minimum of 48 hours. Make sure you dry your gear out of direct sunlight to avoid UV damage.

Rinsing and drying will also help preserve your equipment. In some cases you may want to use a mild soap and warm water to remove dirt, sweat, sunscreen, insect repellent, and salt. You can find soap specifically designed to clean and protect high-tech fabrics, including neoprene, at boating and outdoor stores.

Once your gear is dry, store it in a cool, dark place. If you have space to hang your equipment, great. If you don't, store your paddling gear loosely in a mesh bag or plastic bin. Try not to pack items in too tightly, as over time the material will weaken along folded areas. One trick to keep moisture out of your storage container is to throw in a handful of those silicon drying packets that come with electronics.

CHAPTER FOUR

BASIC PADDLING TECHNIQUE

FOR YOUR FIRST EXCURSION, IT'S A GOOD IDEA TO PICK A MELLOW RIVER or a lake. It's nice to have some current so that you can practice strokes and begin learning to read the water, but if you are a true beginner, getting on a lake first is well worth your time. If you have some river experience, you can hop onto something a little more challenging. Packrafts are a lot more forgiving than a hard-sided kayak, but they are also not as high performing, so give yourself a little time to get used to the different feel, even if you are an experienced boater.

The first thing people notice when they hop into a packraft is that the boat seems to twist and turn with every stroke. Without a keel, these little boats don't track in a straight line very well; instead they spin quickly and easily, making them great for maneuvering through obstacles.

Packrafts are light and have a relatively high profile, so they can be challenging to paddle in strong winds.

These characteristics mean it's a lot more fun to paddle a packraft in moving water downriver than across a big, long, flat lake in a headwind. You can use packrafts for crossing open bodies of water, especially if you have no other option for a craft, but you won't understand people's delight in these fun little boats if your first experience is paddling into the wind on a lake.

Paddling a packraft comes fairly naturally to most people. The rafts are stable, responsive, and forgiving, so you can get by without a lot of paddling skill. But efficient and effective paddling allows you to move your boat with precision, helps conserve energy on long days, and min-

For your first excursions in your packraft, practice your paddling skills on a lake or a flatwater river.

imizes strain on your body, so it's worth developing your skills. Strong strokes are the foundation of your boating and will allow you to tackle challenging obstacles with confidence.

WET EXITS AND ENTRIES

The first thing you should practice is how to get into and out of your packraft on the water. Take your boat to a lake, pond, or swimming pool to test it out. Try flipping first without your spray deck or spray skirt in place, then practice with it on. Get out in water deep enough that you cannot stand, and try to right your boat while dog paddling. Swim with your boat and paddle. The more you play around with what it feels like to be in the water with your boat, the more comfortable you will be if you accidentally come out of your packraft on a river.

The difficulty of exiting your boat when it is upside down depends on the type of packraft you have. In a self-bailing packraft, you will just fall out if your boat tips over. Thigh straps may complicate the exit slightly, but generally you simply need to straighten your legs to release the pressure on the straps, allowing you to drop out of the boat.

If you have a spray deck held in place with Velcro, you will probably fall out of the boat easily as well, since the weight of your body is enough to rip the Velcro apart. If the deck does not come free, stay calm. Bring

With most spray decks on packrafts, you usually just fall out of your boat and pop up alongside it when you tip over.

your hand to your waist, rip the Velcro apart to disconnect it, and then push yourself out of the boat.

Spray skirts are more difficult to release but still aren't hard, especially if you practice a few times. To release a spray skirt, bend forward at the waist and feel for the grab loop on the front of the skirt with one hand while holding your paddle with the other. When you find the loop, pull it up and away to free the elastic from the coaming. This is usually easy to do, but if it's your first time upside down in a boat, it can be challenging to keep your composure. So familiarize yourself with the technique in calm water until you can perform it without thinking. Many experienced boaters have beginners count to ten before they pull the grab loop just to help them relax while they are suspended upside down underwater. Try it. You can hold your breath for a long time if you remain calm.

If you don't fall out of your boat immediately because of your thigh straps or spray skirt, it's important to protect your head while you are upside down. To do this, bend forward at the waist, keeping your face as close to the deck of your packraft as possible. This position will also make it easier for you to reach the grab loop of your spray skirt, if your packraft has one. Make sure you can find your grab loop by feel. Don't rely on your eyes alone to locate the loop—you may be in turbulent or murky water that makes it impossible to see anything.

Wet Exits with Thigh Straps

If you have installed thigh straps in your packraft and do not have any previous whitewater kayaking experience, it's important to practice your wet exits in a pool or on flatwater before you hit the river. Thigh straps can hold you upside down inside your boat as you move downstream, exposing your head to rocks and other underwater obstacles. You need to bend forward at your waist to keep your head close to the packraft and then straighten your legs to release pressure on the thigh straps so you can push yourself out of the boat to exit. Beginners should start out wearing their thigh straps relatively loose to ensure an easy exit in case of a flip.

Once you are free of the spray skirt, push the packraft away as though you were pushing down a pair of pants. This analogy should help keep you bent forward at the waist and minimize your chance of hitting rocks with your head. Think about it: It is impossible to pull down your pants if your back is arched and your head is behind your shoulders. Once free of the boat, your PFD's buoyancy will help bring your head to the surface.

When your head pops out of the water, grab onto your boat as well as your paddle. If you were in a rapid, you'd immediately assume the defensive swimming position—lying on your back with your feet up and downstream of the rest of your body. In a lake this position isn't critical, but it's good to imprint the right habits, so float on your back by your packraft for a minute or two before you move to right it.

Try to flip your packraft over by pushing up on the tube. Packrafts flip pretty easily if they do not have a load on the bow, but it behooves you to practice this self-rescue technique on flatwater before you tackle it in a rapid. If you have a heavy backpack lashed onto the bow, it can be nearly impossible to right your packraft without first swimming to shore.

To right your packraft, push up on the tube.

To get back into your packraft on the water, pull your upper body onto the air tube (top), kick your legs up until they are on the surface of the water, and then kick and pull yourself up and over the tube (center). Once your torso is over the tube, roll so that your butt comes into the raft, then pull your legs down and in front of you (bottom).

When your boat is upright, place your paddle across the tubes, holding onto it with one hand, and kick your legs up until your body is parallel to the surface of the water. You'll probably find this easier to do if you are upstream of your boat. Grab onto the tubes, a grab line, your thigh straps, or the seat—anything you can hang onto—and kick vigorously until you get your belly up and over the side of the packraft tube. Roll over and into the boat. Uprighting your packraft drains out all the water, so you should be ready to continue paddling downstream once you are back in the boat.

PADDLING POSITION

You sit in a packraft the same way you sit in a kayak: upper body perpendicular to the axis of the boat, legs out in front of you, feet braced against the bow, knees partly bent and pressed against the raft tubes. This is termed your power position, as it puts you in a strong paddling position.

As mentioned earlier, many boaters install thigh straps in their packrafts to give them added control. These straps should run around your knees and be cinched down so that they hold your legs comfortably in

Sit up straight in your packraft with your legs extended, knees slightly bent, and feet pressed against the front of the boat.

place. The goal is to enable you to tilt your raft by lifting up the tube with pressure on your leg, which means the thigh straps have to be snug. Snug thigh straps also reduce the chance of entrapment—which is the biggest worry some folks have with them besides their added weight.

Sit up straight in your boat so that when you paddle you can rotate at your waist with each stroke. If you find yourself sinking backward, you can place a small dry bag filled with the things you want to keep handy during the day behind your back to provide extra support. (Make sure you clip the bag in so it won't disappear if you flip.) You can also install a kayak back band like those made by Jackson Kayak. The beauty of this kind of backrest is that you can tighten or loosen it to adjust your position.

You don't always have to have your legs extended. That's your power position, so it sets you up for maneuvering in moving water. If you are just floating downstream, you can relax, cross your legs, or even drape them over the sides of the raft.

HAND POSITION ON THE PADDLE

First pick up your paddle in both hands and place the middle of the shaft on top of your head. If your hands are in the proper position, your arms will be on either side of your head, with your elbows bent at 90 degrees. Have someone check to make sure you are in the right position. If your hands are too close together, it's hard to put much power into your stroke. If they are too far apart, you are likely to tire rapidly, as this position takes more upper body strength to move the paddle through the water.

Grip the paddle loosely. You don't need or want to use a death grip to hold on. Instead press the tip of your index finger against your thumb to create an O shape and let your other fingers fold around the shaft in a relaxed grip. Your knuckles should be pointed up. If you are using a feathered paddle (more on that below), the blade on your strong side will be vertical.

Breakdown paddles generally allow you to adjust the angle between the blades. You can opt to have no angle—or a non-feathered blade—which means you do not need to rotate the paddle between strokes. Or you can opt to create an angle between the two blades to allow you to feather.

A good starting point for determining the width of your hands on your paddle is to hold it on your head with your elbows at 90 degrees. From here you can adjust to what feels comfortable. Many people paddle with too narrow a grip, so this starting point works well. In this photo, the paddle is slightly offset. Try to start with your head positioned in the middle of your paddle.

Feathered paddles cut down on air resistance by rotating the blade as it moves through the air between strokes. Non-feathered blades remain vertical throughout the stroke. Minimizing wind resistance can be important on lakes or open water, but for downriver boating you don't really need to worry about it too much.

Lower-end breakdown paddles generally offer three paddle positions. The ferrule or joint where the paddle is hooked together will have three holes where a button on the other half of the paddle snaps in to lock the paddle in place. These angles are usually 60 degrees to the right, 0 degrees and 60 degrees to the left. Higher-end paddles offer greater adjustability in the angle settings. Most paddlers opt for a 30-degree angle between their blades. Too much more of an angle and your wrist will be cocked too severely.

Hold your paddle with a relaxed grip (top). If you use a death grip, as shown in the bottom photo, you'll tire quickly and may end up with tendonitis or wrist or elbow injuries.

Nonfeathered paddles like the one in this photo are helpful if you have wrist problems and want to minimize the repetitive twisting motion in your wrists that are required to feather.

With a feathered paddle, your control hand rotates the paddle with each stroke, while the paddle simply slides through the grip of the other hand as it feathers. Most right-handed people prefer to use their right hand as the control hand; lefties generally like their left. High-end paddles tend to be predetermined as either a right- or left-control paddle. Adjustable paddles allow you to make a choice. If you don't know your preference, play around with different paddles to see what feels comfortable.

First-time paddlers may want to opt out of feathering until they get their stroke technique down.

THE FORWARD STROKE

Most people can pick up a kayak paddle and intuitively know how to paddle forward. You dip one paddle in the water and then the other, right?

The forward stroke seems pretty basic, but to be effective—and powerful—you want to develop good technique, and that technique isn't necessarily instinctive.

A forward stroke is about more than arm power. Proper technique will allow you to engage your arms, back, abdomen, and leg muscles. Combining these different muscles helps minimize arm and shoulder fatigue and allows you to paddle all day long without tiring.

Step 1: The Catch

For your first stroke, rotate your right shoulder forward and extend your right arm until the paddle blade is close to your feet. "Spear" the water with both hands to submerge the blade into the water. Your left hand should be about shoulder height and your torso twisted so that the right side is angled toward the bow of your boat to give you more reach and set up the torso rotation you need for power. Place your blade into the water around your feet.

Bury your paddle to the top of the blade. The blade's power face should be perpendicular to the direction of travel. Your lower arm should be almost straight. Your upper arm should be relaxed with a slight bend so that your wrist is close to your eyes.

To begin your forward stroke, start with your torso twisted forward toward the front blade of your paddle. Your forward arm is straight. The blade enters the water by your feet. Your upper arm is in a "looking at your wristwatch" position.

Step 2: Power Phase

Begin the paddling stroke by uncoiling your torso, keeping your lower arm straight. Press your stroke-side foot against the packraft tube to support your body. Try to generate power using the strong muscles of your torso rather than relying on your arm strength. Keep your upper arm relaxed so that it gets a bit of a reprieve. Your upper hand should still be at about eye level.

Body rotation is the most important component of a powerful, efficient forward stroke. This rotation involves your entire torso, not just your shoulders. Twist from the lower part of your spine, envisioning a steel rod running up your back to the top of your head. Avoid excessive side-to-side rocking. This causes your packraft to bob up and down and slows you down. If that is happening, quiet your body and focus on coiling and uncoiling your torso.

As your blade moves through the water, your torso unwinds. Keep your lower arm relatively straight.

As you move through the stroke, your body continues to unwind until your shoulders are square to the boat.

Push your upper arm across your body with your elbow bent at 45 degrees, ending with you looking forward across the top of your forearm as though you are checking the time on your wristwatch. Pushing the shaft across the centerline of the boat enables you to keep the paddle as close to vertical in the water as possible.

Paddling Tip

To help ensure that you use rotation to generate power in your forward stroke, imagine that your paddle is frozen in place and you are moving your packraft past the blade rather than pulling the blade through the water.

Step 3: Release and Recovery

The blade exits the water around your hip. You don't gain any power by pulling farther back (the most powerful part of the stroke is up by the feet). Lift your paddle straight out of the water (don't let your elbow bend more than 90 degrees). Your torso and shoulders should be rotated so that your left side is now facing the bow and ready for the catch on the left side of the boat.

Rotate the blade (if feathered) by rolling your control hand forward at the wrist, and spear the blade into the water on the opposite side from your previous stroke.

To become proficient with the forward paddle stroke, practice on flatwater. Try to see how much—or how little—power it takes to propel your boat forward. Experiment with what happens when you take a hard stroke or two on one side. Try planting the paddle as close to the raft tubes as possible. Narrow strokes help keep your boat from swinging side to side with each stroke. Playing around with your strokes helps you learn more about your packraft and how it responds, which will come in handy when you need to maneuver to avoid obstacles.

The blade of your paddle leaves the water around your hip. As the blade exits, your torso should be coiling up in the opposite direction from where you begin the stroke, with the other shoulder pointing forward and your upper hand reaching for the next stroke.

Tips for an Efficient, Powerful Forward Stroke

- Sit up straight.
- Picture your torso as a coiled spring. With each stroke the spring uncoils, releasing energy before winding up for the next stroke on the other side.
- Practice rotation by keeping your arms straight throughout the entire stroke, which means the only way to move the paddle is by moving your torso.
- Relax your fingers on your upper hand to keep them from over-gripping.
- Keep your lower body quiet to avoid rocking your packraft back and forth and decreasing the efficiency of your forward movement.

BACK PADDLING

The back stroke is simply the reverse of the forward stroke, and like the forward stroke, its power is derived from engaging your entire body with torso rotation.

Back paddling helps slow or stop your boat in the current. Packrafts are not very fast boats, even when you are paddling hard. Their high profile and light weight make them susceptible to the wind and easily tossed by waves. Back paddling gives you time to assess what is happening downstream and allows you to move away from rocks or holes.

Back paddling also helps keep you drier when you move through wave trains. Slowing down your boat allows it to rise and fall with the waves rather than slam through them, crashing down into the troughs with water pouring in over the tubes. This is especially important in frigid water, where your comfort and safety require that you stay warm, as well as in an open, non-self-bailing boat, which becomes sluggish and unresponsive if it fills with water. If most of your boating experience has been in a rigid-shell kayak, you may be surprised at how often you will opt to back paddle rather than power forward in your packraft. You'll find a balance as you gain experience.

SWEEP STROKE

Sweeping your blade out and away from the side of your raft turns the boat and allows you to maintain your hard-won velocity. Sweeping on the right side of your boat will turn the bow to the left. Sweeping on the left turns the bow right.

A series of well-executed sweep strokes will turn your boat in a gradual, arcing turn with little loss of momentum.

Step 1: Place the blade in the water by your feet as you would with a forward stroke.

Step 2: Sweep the blade in a wide arc toward the stern, reaching out and away from the raft to make a half circle with the paddle blade. Make sure to rotate to get the maximum arc. The most powerful part of the arc is the first and last 20 or 30 degrees, where the paddle is close to the boat but pulling away from the bow or drawing into the stern.

To initiate a sweep stroke, wind up your torso so the shoulder and hand on the stroke side of your packraft are pointing forward. Place the blade in the water as far forward and close to the boat as possible.

As your blade catches the water, unwind your torso like an explosive spring and arc your blade away from the side of the packraft.

As your blade arcs away from the side of your packraft, turn your head so that you are looking in the direction the boat is moving. Begin uncoiling your torso so that your shoulders begin to square with the boat.

Your paddle should be as close to horizontal as you can make it, so both hands will be low as opposed to a forward stroke, where the top hand is about eye level.

Step 3: Lift the paddle out of the water when it comes close to the back side of your boat. *Note:* You will keep your blade in the water longer for a sweep stroke than for a forward stroke.

Practice doing full sweeps from the front of your boat to the back of the boat. Once you have a feel for that, do a series of half sweeps—front to side (ending out from the hip) and side to back (starting out from the hip).

Sweeps can also be done as back sweeps; just reverse how you are doing the front sweep. A sweep on the right side followed by a back sweep on the left will really get you turning. You do not flip your paddle over for a reverse stroke or sweep. Simply use the back side of the blade as your strong side during the stroke.

On a forward sweep your blade leaves the water near the stern of the packraft. Notice how the paddler in this photo has recoiled his body so that he is ready to take a stroke on the opposite side of the boat.

Sweep–Forward Stroke Combo

You may find you have trouble keeping your boat straight when you are paddling forward. Often paddlers veer away from their strong side or the current, and wind can push boats one way or the other. You can correct with a sweep stroke, but that may cause more correction than you need. This is where blending a forward stroke and a sweep stroke can help.

If you find yourself moving toward one side, start with a sweep rather than a forward stroke on the side you are veering toward. As the boat straightens, raise your outside hand to bring the paddle back to vertical, which will bring the blade close to the side of the boat, transforming the sweep into a forward stroke.

If you are ending a forward stroke and your packraft is still heading in the wrong direction, you can add the end of a sweep to your stroke. Instead of taking the blade out of the water at your hip, push it away from the side of your packraft by dropping your upper hand so that the paddle

A reverse sweep starts with the blade near the stern of the packraft and the torso twisted back so that the shoulder on the downward side is pointing toward the rear of the boat (top). As the torso unwinds, the upper hand stays close to the chest, creating a pivot point for the packraft. The blade stays completely immersed (center). The blade comes out of the water close to the bow (bottom).

moves from a vertical to a more horizontal position, and then sweep or draw it into the stern to correct the orientation of the boat.

Don't expect to master this technique right away. It takes time to develop a sense of how the boat is going to move, how to react to change directions, and how much to react to make the appropriate correction; but with time and practice, you will find your paddling gets smoother.

One good exercise is to pick an object in the distance and try to paddle straight toward it. Go easy, and use good strokes and stroke combinations. With time you will find that going straight becomes easier and easier to do.

DRAW STROKE

Draw strokes are used to move your boat sideways, allowing you to pull into a dock, up to another boat, or away from an obstacle.

Twist your torso toward the side of your packraft and reach out as far from the boat as possible with your lower hand. The blade should enter the water around your hip and be fully immersed. Keep your upper hand close to your head, where it will become a pivot point for the paddle.

Hold your upper hand steady, pulling the blade toward you with your lower hand.

When the blade comes close to the side of the packraft, you can either remove it by pulling it up and out of the water or feather the blade and slice it through the water and away from the boat for another draw stroke.

Step 1: Place your paddle blade into the water about 2 feet from the side of your packraft, with the blade facing or parallel to the boat and the shaft at a slight angle from the water to your upper hand.

Step 2: Pull the blade toward you with your lower hand, straightening the shaft until your upper hand is above your lower one. Be careful not to bring the blade all the way into the boat (see Catching a Crab).

Step 3: Without removing the blade from the water, turn it 90 degrees by cocking your wrist forward, and slice the blade through the water and back out to your starting point. Rotate the blade until it is parallel to the boat and draw it in again, repeating the process until your boat is where you want it. Alternatively, once you have drawn the blade in toward the boat slide it forward or back to remove it from the water so you can initiate some other stroke.

BRACING

A brace can help keep you from capsizing when you get hit by a wave, get sucked into a hole, or lean the wrong way on an eddy line. In a kayak, a brace involves three things: a paddle slap on the water, a hip snap, and getting your head down. In a packraft, a hip snap is less effective, especially if you don't have thigh straps. What is important is having the correct body position. You want to curl over toward the downward side—or the side that is going under—of your boat in a C shape, with your head low to your shoulder. As you brace off the water, your body will straighten up with the boat.

Catching a Crab

At times you may feel as though your blade is getting sucked under the boat. Boaters call this "catching a crab." Don't force the blade back to the surface if you feel this pressure. Catching a crab can cause your boat to flip. Instead let go with your upper hand to remove pressure from the blade. After the blade slips back to the surface, grab it and start over.

The wonderful thing about packrafts is that they don't flip over as easily as a kayak or canoe. You have those nice fat air tubes surrounding you that do not get sucked underwater easily. That said, big-enough water features can still cause you to flip, and some older-style packrafts are prone to flipping backward. Being able to brace and redistribute your body weight can keep you upright when you feel the boat upending.

Water pushing down on your upstream tube is the most common way to flip a packraft. This can happen whenever you encounter variations in current and your direction of travel, such as when you cross an eddy line or end up in a hole.

Your body position is critical to staying upright. If you find yourself getting pulled down to one side, curl over toward that downward tube to get your weight low. If you have thigh straps, you can pull up on the downward leg by snapping your hips in an attempt to bring the tube up from beneath the water. In the absence of thigh straps, the more important way to keep upright is to bring your head and torso down toward the side you are righting and to brace with your paddle.

This movement seems counterintuitive to most beginner boaters, and the first few times you will undoubtedly lean away from the side of the boat that is headed down. In doing so, you raise your center of gravity upward. Since the boat is already unstable and headed over, leaning the wrong way creates more leverage for the water to flip you over. By dropping your head toward the water, the center of gravity is decreased, making it more likely the water will release the side of the boat and start flowing under it again.

If you have thigh straps, you can get a sense of how this feels by lining your raft up next to a dock or having someone stand in the water next to you so that you can push off his or her hands while you practice. Tilt your boat on edge and then flatten it back out by snapping your hips up and away from the downside tube. Drop your head and torso down at the same time, creating a C shape between your hip and your head that opens toward the downside. Once the boat is righted, you can sit up again, bringing your head up last.

Body position is critical to an effective brace, so it's worth practicing until you get a sense of how it works.

Without thigh straps, it's virtually impossible to perform a hip snap. But it's still important to think about where your weight is in the boat. If you find yourself being pulled over, bend your torso over toward the downside tube, regardless of whether you can pull against a strap.

Low versus High Brace

The main difference between a low and high brace is the orientation of your paddle as it comes into contact with the surface of the water. With a high brace, the power face of your blade hits the water. With a low brace, it's the opposite—the back side of the blade slaps the water. The power face of your paddle is the one pointing back toward the stern of your boat as you paddle. There's some debate about which brace—high or low—is more effective in a packraft. Some packrafters think it's the high brace; others favor the low. We go into more details about the pros and cons of each below.

To perform a high brace, roll your wrist back so that the power face of the blade faces down and slap the surface of the water. Keep your upper hand low and close to your body to protect your shoulder.

High Brace

With the high brace, you need to bring the power face of your blade in contact with the water surface. To do this, roll your wrist backward so that your knuckles face the stern of your raft. Slap the water with your blade. As the boat rights itself, curl over toward the downside tube and drop your head. Once the boat is flat, straighten your body. Remember, your head comes up last. When the boat stabilizes, you can move into whatever stroke is appropriate to get you going again.

High braces have a reputation for causing shoulder injuries, but actually it's improperly performed high braces that are the problem. For an effective, safe high brace, keep your elbows close to your side. This protects your shoulder and keeps you in a powerful ready position in case the waves keep coming at you.

Low Brace

Low braces are used less frequently than high braces by packrafters because the height of the tubes can make it difficult to use one effectively, especially if you are on the small side. If you sit low in your packraft, you have to have your elbows quite high to clear the boat's tubes and bring the back side of your paddle blade down onto the water with enough power to keep your boat from flipping.

That said, many boaters use the low brace all the time and are big fans of its effectiveness in helping them stay upright. Your choice may

Author's Tip

Most beginner boaters run into trouble with their braces because their hands are not in the correct position on their paddle. If you are holding your paddle incorrectly, when you roll your paddle to make it parallel to the water, you may end up with it at an angle, causing it to dive under the water when you attempt your brace. Obviously, a diving paddle is not going to give you any support, and you are likely to tip over if that happens. Make sure you keep your hands in the proper orientation on your paddle at all times so that you know what will happen to your paddle if you cock your wrist forward or back.

be dictated by your size and position in your packraft. For taller paddlers who sit higher in the boat, a low brace could be effective. For smaller boaters the opposite might be true. If you are a beginner packrafter, it's probably best to focus on the high brace. As you gain skill, you can add the low brace to your repertoire.

A low brace is performed by rolling your knuckles forward toward the bow of your boat and slapping the water with the back side of your blade. Your elbows will be up and the paddle shaft low and close to your body. Keep the shaft horizontal and as close to the deck of your packraft as possible. This can be challenging if you are small, and you may need to angle the shaft for the blade to make contact with the water, but your goal is to keep it low.

The brace stops the packraft from capsizing, at least temporarily. To upright your boat, you'll need to follow up the brace with a good curled body position, head down, followed by a hip snap if you are using thigh straps.

In general, low braces aren't used as much in packrafting as they are in hard-sided kayaks, but they can be an effective way to keep upright. To perform a low brace, roll your knuckles forward and slap the water with the back side of your blade.

Low braces can be used when your boat has barely tipped. It's a quick defensive reaction that protects your shoulders and helps keep boaters in the correct, neutral body position. Some paddlers even float through rough water hanging out in the low brace position between their active forward strokes.

FERRYING

Ferries are critical for maneuvering your boat from one side of a river to the other without losing ground. They help set you up for rapids, get you over to eddies, or help you reach a camp or takeout on the opposite side of the river. Once you have perfected your ferry angle, you'll be amazed how quickly you can shoot across the current.

To ferry you need to angle your boat to the current as you paddle across. The current will carry you downstream if you simply point your raft at the opposite bank and start paddling. If you angle your boat upstream, your strokes counter the pull of the water, drawing you across without losing ground.

It takes practice to figure out what angle works best for any given situation. In general, the more upstream you face, the slower you'll move laterally, and the more your paddle strokes will be working to keep you from drifting downstream rather than moving you to the other side of the river. As you increase your angle and point more across the current, you'll move more quickly across and use less power to keep from drifting downstream. But in a powerful river, too much angle can cause you to be carried farther by the current.

We'll go into more detail about how to begin your ferry in whitewater when we talk about exiting and entering eddies later in this chapter. For now let's discuss ferrying in the context of a moving river without obstacles or waves to contend with. To start, face upstream with your bow pointing about 45 degrees off the flow of the current. You can play with the exact angle as you practice your ferry to see what works best.

Think about tilting your raft slightly downstream so that the upstream tube is lifted and can't catch in the current. With thigh straps you can actually get your packraft on edge; without them just shift your weight to the downstream side of your boat for the tilt.

Paddle forward, maintaining the 45-degree angle as you shoot across the stream. Keep an eye on your target so that you can adjust your angle. If you find yourself drifting downstream too much, turn your boat so that you are pointing more upstream. If you find you are actually moving upstream of your destination, ease off on the angle and let the current carry you more. Pay attention to your paddling. Sometimes you'll only have to set your ferry angle and the current will carry you across without much effort. Other times you'll have to paddle hard to hold the angle and make progress against the current.

Back Ferry

The only downside to the ferry described above is that your back is facing downstream, making it hard to see obstacles below. That can be problematic if you need to see a hazard. It is also harder to do on the fly, because you have to turn your boat around. But an upstream-facing ferry is much more powerful than a back ferry, and so is best suited for use when you need to cross the entire river without moving downstream.

Back ferries allow you to reposition your boat and avoid obstacles. Angle your stern roughly 45 degrees off the main current and back paddle until you position your packraft where you want it.

On the fly, a back ferry is a good way to reposition your boat as you move downstream. The principles are the same except that now your stern will be facing upstream and you will be back paddling to position your packraft. Again, angle the stern roughly 45 degrees off the current and tilt downstream slightly to lift the upstream tube. Back paddle, keeping close track of your position so that you can adjust your angle as necessary.

Practice ferrying until you feel confident in your ability to use this technique with precision and control. Ferrying is a critical boating skill and can keep you out of trouble and away from hazards, so be sure it's part of your paddling repertoire.

EDDY TURNS

Eddies form on the downstream side of an obstruction. The obstruction slows and twists the water, causing it to turn and flow upstream behind the obstacle. Eddies are found along the sides of the river, below bends, and downstream of rocks or other obstacles. The water in an eddy can be calm or, in big water, can be swirling and violent. Packrafters use eddies as a place to pull out of the main current of the river to scout, exit the boat, rest, or regroup. Being able to exit and enter eddies with confidence and ease is a critical boating skill.

Eddy Exits or Peel Outs

The line between the river's main current and the eddy is called the eddy line or eddy fence. Eddy lines can be turbulent and powerful and require power to punch through. Smaller eddy lines take less aggression to breach, but the principles for crossing them are the same.

Your goal is to cross the eddy line where it is most defined, which is usually at the top of the eddy, just below the obstacle that created it. Lower down the eddy line spreads out, creating a wider area of swirling water that can be harder to cross. Some eddies peter out at their lower end, allowing boaters to slip out the bottom. But don't cheat on every eddy by sneaking out. Learning to enter and exit eddies is an essential river-running skill.

To leave an eddy, start paddling upstream so that you have time to build up your speed. Aim to hit the top of the eddy line at a 45-degree

Angle your boat roughly 45 degrees to the main current eddy line and paddle toward the top of the eddy (top). As your boat hits the eddy line, paddle hard, powering through the eddy line (bottom).

When the bow of your packraft crosses into the main current, do a sweep stroke on the upstream side of your boat (top). Look downstream to help tilt your boat, which will pivot around when the main current catches the bow. Once you are in the main flow of the river, paddle away (bottom).

angle. Paddle hard. As your boat moves into the main current, tilt your packraft downstream to lift your upstream tube up off the water. This ensures that the main current will come in under the tube and help spin your boat downstream and into the main current. If you don't tilt your packraft downstream, your upstream tube can get sucked under as you enter the current, flipping your boat.

As your packraft crosses the eddy line, do a sweep on the eddy side of the boat and then stick your downstream blade into the main current near your feet in the same position you would use for a draw stroke (blade parallel to the raft, shaft angled down toward the water, upstream hand about eye level). Imagine that you are catching the current with your blade. Your boat will pivot around your blade until it faces downstream. Once you are out of the eddy, resume paddling downriver.

Practice exiting eddies on both sides. Eddies on the right side of the river call for a right tilt on both the entrance and the exit. Eddies on the left take a left lean when you come in and out of them.

River Left and River Right

When boaters talk about the different sides of a river, they use the terms "river right" and "river left," with right and left referring to your perspective as you paddle downstream. River left always means *your* left as you face downriver. River right is always to your right, facing downstream.

Entering an Eddy or Eddy Turns

To enter an eddy, you simply reverse the process described for exiting. As you paddle downstream, look for eddies in the lee of boulders, outcroppings, and bends. Aim for the point where the obstacle meets the main current. That will be the top of the eddy line.

Paddle hard toward that point, angling your boat 45 degrees to the current. Punch through the eddy line, tilting your boat into your turn so that your downstream tube is lifted up. Remember, the downstream tube will actually be upstream of the current in the eddy because the water

Angle your packraft 45 degrees from the top of the eddy, and paddle hard toward it (top). As your feet cross the eddy line, look to the top of the eddy to help tilt your boat properly (bottom).

Reach your upstream hand forward to place a stroke in the eddy (top). As your packraft moves into the upstream current in the eddy, it will swing around, pivoting on the blade of your paddle (bottom). Once your boat is rotated and in the slack water of the eddy, you can hang out until it is time to move on downstream.

there is flowing in the opposite direction from the main river. As your bow crosses the eddy line, sweep on the downriver side and then draw or brace your paddle on the opposite side in the eddy's current to pull your boat around and into the eddy.

Leaving an Eddy to Do a Ferry

Often your goal in leaving an eddy may be to get to the other side of the river. In this case you may not want to do an eddy turn that will take you downstream right away, but instead want to set yourself up for a ferry. To do this, paddle up to the eddy line at about a 45-degree angle with as much speed as you can muster. As you cross the eddy line, sweep on the downriver side of your packraft to keep it facing upstream. Once across the eddy line, set your ferry angle to take you across the river.

PIROUETTE OR SPIN

A pirouette is a rapid spin of the packraft executed by either a sweep or a draw stroke. The pirouette helps you avoid obstacles and is a technique commonly used by whitewater rafters, but it also works for certain pack-raft models. Newer packrafts with pointy bows and sterns and flat hulls (similar in shape to an inflatable kayak) do not pirouette or spin as readily as older stubby packrafts or packrafts with a rocker, like the BAKraft. Play around with your packraft to see how well it spins. You may find this to be a useful trick for navigating tight rock gardens.

PRACTICE, PRACTICE, PRACTICE

Paddling strokes, ferrying, wet exits and entrances, spins, and eddy turns are critical river-running skills. You can get by without them on easy water, but as soon as you begin to tackle rivers with obstacles and rough water, you need to rely on these techniques to be safe. Practice until you are bored and never want to make another ferry or eddy turn. Only then will you know you have these skills hard-wired.

CHAPTER FIVE

READING WATER

ALL WATER FLOWS DOWNHILL, SEEKING THE MOST DIRECT, STEEPEST, and clearest route in its path to the sea. That flow is known as current. Keep this principle in mind as you look at a river. Often knowing where the most current is flowing will help you determine the best, most efficient path to paddle downstream.

The current's speed or velocity is determined by a river's volume, width, and gradient or steepness of the riverbed. River volume is mea-

Knowing how to read the river helps you pick the safest, cleanest lines through obstacles. This paddler is following a tongue of water that indicates a channel through a line of rocks, while his partner spots from a downstream eddy.

River constriction and rock obstacles create a rapid downstream of a relatively calm pool.

sured according to cubic feet per second, or cfs, which refers to how many cubic feet of water move past a given point in a second.

Narrow river corridors constrict water, forcing it to pile up into waves and flow faster. As the river's currents converge in tight canyons, you often find turbulence. Wider rivers typically have calmer, slower water.

Rapids generally occur when the river gradient steepens, the current accelerates, the channel narrows, or the river bottom is rough. Flat pools have less gradient and deeper, slower-moving water.

Water moves slower along the riverbed than on the surface because of friction. This differentiation is known as laminar flow. You also have friction along the sides of the river, where the difference in the current's speed creates helical flow, or spiraling swirls of slower-moving water. This water gets pulled into the faster water in the middle of the river and then twists down toward the bottom of the river before being drawn back to the shore. You can see this effect when you drop a twig into the river close to shore and watch as it gets pulled out into the main current and sucked under.

RIVER BENDS

When the river bends, the main current is forced to the outside of the bend. Here the water will be deeper and faster than on the inside of the turn. Water piles up on the outside of the bend, cutting into the riverbank and depositing debris. Strainers or fallen trees are often found on the outside of bends.

Water on the inside of a bend moves slower and is shallower than on the outside. Sometimes the water is too shallow to boat in, although packrafts can float across pretty shallow water. You can recognize shallow water by riffles and exposed gravel or rocks.

CHANNELS

Channels are formed when water collides with obstacles, such as boulders, and is forced to move around the obstacle to make its way downhill. In deeper water these channels form a V or tongue of smooth water on

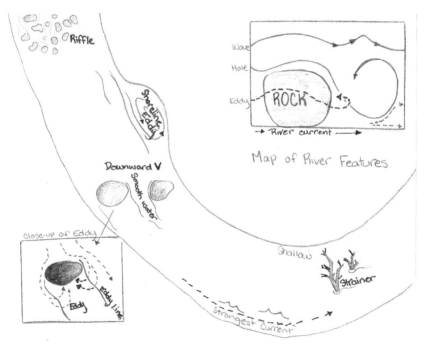

AVERY ABSOLON

Channels can often be identified by a smooth—or V-shaped—tongue of water that flows between obstacles.

the surface. Often river runners look for these Vs as a safe path through shallow water or past rocks.

ROCKS

A rock that projects above the surface of the water forces the current to flow around it, creating an eddy downstream. Such eddies can be a good spot to stop, regroup, and look over your shoulder for other obstacles downstream.

When water flows over a rock that lies just beneath the surface, it forms a "pillow" of smooth, glassy water. You may also see an upside-down V downstream of a rock. Unlike a normal V that indicates a channel, the upside-down V indicates a submerged obstacle that is diverting the flow of the current. In packrafts with a shallow draft, you can often float over submerged rocks, but beware—these hidden obstacles can also pin your boat if the rock is too close to the surface. In general, avoid upside-down Vs.

Eddies formed behind midstream rocks make a good place to stop and regroup before continuing downstream.

When water runs into an obstacle like this rock, it piles up on itself, forming a pillow. You can tell this rock is not undercut on its upstream side because of the amount of water pillowing up against it.

Water also pillows up against rocks that break the river surface. These pillows are frothy and turbulent. They show that the water has hit a solid obstacle and is piling up and collapsing down around the edges to continue its way downstream. Undercut rocks will not have a big pillow because much of the water flows under the obstacle rather than around it. Undercut rocks are extremely dangerous, so it's important to be able to recognize them.

WAVES

Water speeds up as it flows over submerged boulders or is constricted in a narrowing channel and then stacks up downstream into standing waves. As you increase a river's volume and velocity, these waves get bigger and can form a line of waves called a wave train. Waves remain stationary in the river, although the water molecules themselves continue moving downstream. Paddling through a bouncy wave train can be like an exciting roller-coaster ride. But make sure you know the waves are not hiding any rocks or holes that could cause you problems, and if you are paddling

Breaking waves like this one tend to be symmetrical and have a front and a back side.

In busy sections of water, it takes practice to detect rocks and holes before you are on top of them. When you are first learning, it can be helpful to stop and get off the water to look at what's happening downstream before you commit to it.

an open boat, be careful not to ship in too much water. A raft full of water will be sluggish and difficult to maneuver.

Novices often have a hard time differentiating waves from holes or frothy water piling up against a rock. Classic waves are symmetrical and have a front and a back side. Boaters look for glassy waves with smooth green faces to surf. But not all waves are as obvious. Waves can fold back on themselves and break, creating a frothy pile that looks a lot like a rock or hole. You can usually distinguish rocks from standing waves by the shape and character of the wave. Irregular waves or waves that look lower and frothier on the downstream side are generally hiding rocks. The rock may be obvious if you scout the rapid from shore. If you aren't sure, avoid the wave.

ROCK GARDENS

Sections of river with lots of boulders scattered throughout are called rock gardens. Often rock gardens become most apparent at low water, when the normal channels get pinched off as the water levels drop. It can be hard to find a clean line through a rock garden. Packrafts tend to fare better in rock gardens than hard-sided crafts because you can bump off obstacles and spin in tight spots; plus your boat is small and has a very shallow draft. Draft is the minimum depth of water a boat can navigate without getting grounded. Even in a packraft, if the water volume is low

Rocks scattered throughout the river create rock gardens that don't always have one clear path through them. At lower water, rock gardens become trickier to navigate.

and the rocks are close together, you may have to scrape and bump your way over the top of a rock or two to navigate a tight rock garden.

HOLES

Holes are made when water flows over an obstacle, creating a depression below. The obstacles are usually on or near the river surface and often cannot be seen. Instead you see the frothing white foam of turbulent water. The river naturally refills the depression created by the obstacle by folding in on itself and moving back upstream in a recirculating flow, much like an eddy.

If there is enough water recirculating, the hole can become a *keeper hole* that traps and holds solid objects like boats in place. Holes can be fun to play in or paddle through, or they can be violent and rough and can easily cause you to capsize.

Boaters say that *smiling holes*, or holes where the sides point downstream, are safer to play in because they have definite exit points and you

Keeper holes, like this nasty one formed downstream of a pour-over rock, are hard to get out of. You can identify a keeper hole by the way its ends are upstream of the main frothing water.

Holes can be fun obstacles to paddle through, especially when, like this one, there's a lot of current continuing downstream so that you won't get caught in recirculating water.

If you hit a hole sideways and lean the wrong way, you are likely to get "window-shaded" and flip. Here the paddler is leaning into the main current, which drops his tube below the water, causing him to flip.

get flushed downstream if you come out of your boat. *Frowning holes*, where the sides point upstream, or frown, tend to be more difficult to get out of. As you travel to the edge of a frowning keeper hole, you find yourself pushed back into the middle. If you come out of your boat, you may be trapped in the churning water. Frowning holes are best avoided, especially when you are first learning.

Even if you are an expert, remember that a dangerous hole is still a dangerous hole and can trap you. If you get caught in a keeper hole, often the only way out is to come out of your boat and dive down so you can swim below the churning currents that are holding you in place. If you cannot determine whether a hole is dangerous, skip it.

LOW-HEAD DAMS

Low-head dams run across a river channel, creating a barrier. At certain water levels the current flows over such dams, making them look safe to drop. Low-head dams are hazardous, however. A dam doesn't have to be

Low-head dams are hazardous, often having a recirculating hole at the base that can trap boaters.

high to cause problems. Water going over the dam creates a recirculating hole at its base. But unlike a hole formed by a boulder, there is no side to the hole below a dam. Boaters can get caught in the back current, flipped, and trapped. Many boaters have drowned in the turbulence below a low-head dam. Often low-head dams are not marked, so talk to people about the rivers you plan to run, and scout ahead when your vision is obstructed.

BUMPING INTO OBSTACLES

Inevitably you will run into rocks and other obstacles on your way downstream. The beauty of a packraft is that it tends to bounce right off. Many beginner boaters have pinballed their way down a rapid during their early years of paddling. That's fine. It takes time to be able to see all the rocks ahead of you, especially in shallow rivers.

Colliding with a rock can cause you to pin or tip your raft, however, so it's important to know what to do when you hit one. Our natural reaction is to lean away from an obstacle we are about to collide with. Unfortunately that is the wrong reaction. Leaning away drops your

If, like this packrafter, you lean away when you collide with an obstacle, your upstream tube gets sucked under the current, either pinning you against the rock or causing you to flip.

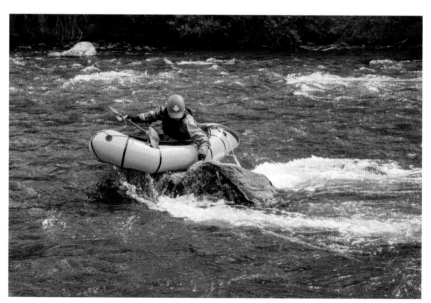

If you bump into a rock, lean into it so that your upstream tube stays up out of the current, allowing you to pivot around and off the obstacle and back into the main flow of the river.

upstream tube and allows water to flow over it, forcing it down and lifting the downstream tube up and onto the obstacle. You could end up stuck on that obstacle—or upside down in the river if your packraft flips.

Instead, lean into the rock. This keeps your upstream tube up and out of the current and allows your raft to simply bump into and slide off the rock, sending you on downstream unscathed.

STRAINERS

Strainers pose a significant hazard to all boaters. A strainer can be created by any number of things—a fallen tree, a logjam, stray branches, a dock—anything that lets water, but not objects like paddlers or boats, flow through. A boater caught against a strainer is like a fish caught in a net or pasta left in a colander. Anything bigger than the holes will be held in place by the relentless force of the current rushing downstream.

Strainers are created when high water from floods or spring runoff eats away at riverbanks, undercutting them on the outside of bends

Fallen trees and logjams create hazards called strainers. Because current continues to flow through the strainer—much like a colander—you can get pinned against them and be unable to escape.

If the current is not too strong, you can ferry across the river above a strainer like this logjam to an open channel or a place where you can get out of your boat and portage around the obstacle. Be wary, however; if you cannot maintain your position and are getting pushed into the obstacle, abort the effort and head for shore.

until they collapse, bringing trees down with them. Sometimes the tree's roots remain connected to the bank and the resulting strainer is called a sweeper. Strainer or sweeper, these hazards can be deadly.

You should always be on the lookout for strainers, especially when you are paddling on an unknown wilderness river. Remember that they are most often found on the outside of bends, so keep your eyes open. The best way to tackle strainers is to avoid them. How? Don't run rivers in flood stage. Scout. Stay alert, particularly as you come upon bends.

If you see a strainer ahead, move away. Sometimes you'll be forced to portage. Other times you can ferry across the river to an open channel. Don't try to squeeze through a space in the strainer, especially in a packraft. Strainers are a double danger for packrafters. A sharp stick can puncture your boat.

What do you do if, despite all your best efforts, you find yourself being swept into a strainer? Your best bet is to lean downstream and grab it. Forget about your paddle and your boat. Haul yourself on top of the strainer. If you can, get out of the water onto the log or tree trunk. If you cannot, concentrate on keeping your head above water and scream for help.

FOLLOW THE LEADER

The line you run through a rapid depends on your skill level. Beginner boaters should look for the cleanest line with the fewest objective hazards and requiring a minimum number of difficult maneuvers to navigate. Advanced boaters tend to look for more challenging lines and features like holes or waves to surf.

Often the best way for a beginner to learn to read water is to follow a more experienced boater through rapids. The mother duck—or experienced boater—picks the line and demonstrates the maneuvers needed to paddle through the rapid efficiently. Mother ducking works best when the beginner boaters are close behind their leader. This enables them to watch their guide carefully and to mimic each paddle stroke.

In mellow water, make note of what obstacles look like as you pass them so that you begin to familiarize yourself with the characteristics of different features.

One of the best ways to learn to read water is to follow a more experienced paddler through a rapid.

Whitewater Ratings

The international rating system for whitewater rapids ranges from Class I to Class VI. The scale is helpful, but deceiving. Rating a rapid is subjective, and the character of a river varies depending on its water level and the type of boat you are using. You may also find regional variations in the way the scale is interpreted and used, meaning that in some places a Class III can feel more like a Class IV or vice versa depending on who came up with the original rating.

Whitewater can be fun and challenging in a packraft, but it's important to understand the difficulty of the rapids before you launch into them unprepared.

SCOUTING RAPIDS

The best way to learn to read water and run rapids is to scout them. Scouting is also critical in difficult water or whenever you come to a horizon line or blind curve where you don't know or can't see what is downstream. Scouting helps keep you out of trouble and allows you to learn to identify safe lines through turbulent water.

Another factor to consider is whether the river is a "pool-drop" river or one continuous rapid. It's a lot easier to run a difficult rapid if you know you have a pool at the bottom rather than miles of raging whitewater with no eddy or calm water in sight. Difficult, technical rivers pose greater threats to swimmers, as do rivers with undercut rocks or lots of downed wood creating strainers. Be conservative, especially if the water is cold or the river is remote.

The International Scale of River Difficulty classifies moving water as follows:

- **Class I:** Moving water with a few riffles and small waves. Few or no obstructions.
- **Class II:** Easy rapids with small waves and clear obvious channels that do not require scouting. Some maneuvering may be required.
- **Class III:** Rapids with high, irregular waves and narrow passages that require precise maneuvering.
- **Class IV:** Long, difficult rapids with constricted channels that require complex maneuvering in turbulent water. The line through the rapid can be hard to determine, and scouting is usually required.
- **Class V:** Extremely long, technical, and violent rapids with tight channels that need to be scouted from shore. Paddlers need to be able to make many precise, intricate moves in turbulent water to negotiate Class V rapids successfully. Rescue conditions are difficult, and there is significant hazard to life in the event of a mishap.
- **Class VI:** Class V rapids on steroids. Class VI water is nearly impossible to navigate, dangerous, and potentially life threatening if something goes wrong. Experts only.

Some river guidebooks will indicate whether it is best to scout a rapid on one side of the river or the other. Often, however, you won't have that information. Simply pull off the river in an eddy upstream of the rapid in question. Make sure the eddy is easy to get into and out of. You don't want to find yourself in trouble in the eddy with a raging rapid just below. If in doubt, pull out higher upriver rather than wait until you are just

The difficulty of a rapid depends on the number and difficulty of maneuvers required to negotiate it successfully and the consequences of a mistake.

above a rapid to scout. You may have to walk a bit farther to check things out, but you won't run the risk of missing your eddy turn and getting carried into the rapid unprepared.

Pull your raft onshore. Packrafts are light and catch the wind easily. If you plan to leave the boat while you scout, tie it down.

For bigger rapids, it's a good idea to carry a throw rope with you while you scout. That way if someone slips and falls into the river, you can help the person get out. Also, you may decide to place spotters along the riverbank to watch while your party negotiates the rapid. These spotters should be armed with a throw rope to assist anyone who gets in trouble.

Wear your PFD and helmet while you scout to protect you in case you fall into the river.

Rapids change dramatically with your perspective. From above you can see things that you cannot see from your boat, but you also get a skewed picture of what the rapid will be like when you are on the water. That means you need to scout from above to get an overall picture of the

Packrafters, armed with throw bags and wearing their helmets and PFDs in case of a mishap, discuss a rapid and look for their line.

It's important to get down near packraft level to get a better idea of what the rapid will look like when you are in your boat.

rapid and then get down to river level so that you can tell what it will look like when you are in your boat.

Find a high point that gives you a good view of the entire rapid. Look carefully at the entrance. Walk down to the end of the rapid to look at where you'll exit the whitewater. Get down to river level so that you can get a sense of what things will look like when you are in your boat. Often rapids look much easier from above than they do at eye level.

As you identify your line, pick out unique features that will help orient you when you are running the rapid. Such landmarks can include distinctive boulders, overhanging trees, a prominent green tongue of water, or a bend in the river. These landmarks help you recognize places in the rapid where you need to make a move or be in a particular place, hazards you have to avoid, and where you want to be as you exit the bottom.

Visualize your route, using the landmarks you've picked out to help you remember what to do at each point. When you are first learning, it helps to go through your visualization verbally with a friend. For example, you'd say, "I'll enter the rapid river right close to the long black rock. After

Before committing to the current, take time to commit the rapid to memory and mentally rehearse the moves you'll be required to make.

the rock, move toward the center of the river. When I see the big square boulder midstream, look for the V on its right side and paddle hard into the V. Hit the wave train, paddling hard to maintain momentum."

While you are scouting a difficult rapid and able to get a look at the whole river, take a minute to think about what might happen if you fail to make a critical move. You should only run rapids you know you will be safe swimming if you make a mistake, especially when you are first starting out. If you are unsure you can do a required maneuver and you don't like the looks of a swim, walk the rapid. The beauty of a packraft is that it is easy to portage, so walking a rapid is no big deal.

Boat Scouting

On easier rivers and in moderate pool-drop rapids, you can sometimes scout from your boat. The best boat scouting technique is to eddy hop your way down the rapid, moving from one safe zone to another, so that you can look downstream and pick out your next maneuver. Sometimes you can just back paddle to slow your packraft and gain enough time to

For easier rapids, you can hop your way downstream from eddy to eddy, stopping to look at what's coming up and planning your next move while paused in an eddy.

Learning to read water and pick your line through obstacles takes time and practice. Start easy.

assess the river ahead before forging on downstream. If you come to a horizon line or a blind corner, you should stop, get out of your boat, and stand up so you can see clearly what lies below. Don't charge ahead unless you know what the river is like and are confident you will not meet any unexpected hazards.

PRACTICE, PRACTICE, PRACTICE

Learning to read water and run rapids is like learning a language. It takes time to recognize different river features and to understand how those features affect your boat. It takes time to learn how to pick a good line through whitewater and to understand the consequences of a mistake. And finally it takes time to gain a healthy respect for the power of water. So practice and find someone who can be your mother duck while you learn.

SCOUT

Use the mnemonic SCOUT to ensure you are methodical and thorough when you scout a rapid.

Section: How many sections are there to this rapid, and where do I want to be for each section?

Current: Where is the main current going in each section? Which current do I want to be on?

Obstacles: What obstacles—trees, rocks, etc.—do I need to be aware of?

Undercuts: Are there places I could get pinned or rocks I could get pulled under?

Talk: About safety and how you are going to run the rapid.

CHAPTER SIX

PUTTING IT ALL TOGETHER

Once you've practiced your strokes, it's time to get on the river. Start with an easy Class I or II section of water, and take your time playing to get a sense of how your packraft responds to your paddling and the current.

COMMUNICATION ON THE RIVER

Out on the river it can be hard to communicate with your colleagues. The sound of the water and the distance between boats make talking—even

The best part about packrafting is getting out and exploring wildlands in a new way. Here packrafters float through Canyonlands National Park.

yelling—almost impossible. For this reason, it is important to discuss your plans onshore or in an eddy, where everyone in your group can hear one another easily.

Decision making in the absence of a designated leader can be tricky. Sometimes your group will have one or two people whose skill level and experience naturally give their opinions more weight. Other times you will all be peers with a similar experience base. If you are faced with hard decisions about what to do or how to run a section of whitewater, it's important to make sure you hear everyone out. Take your time. Listen carefully to people's concerns, and be respectful of other opinions. Once a decision has been made, make sure everyone knows exactly what was decided and is comfortable with the plan.

When you are new to packrafting, ask questions and be sure to speak up if you are worried or afraid. Do not feel compelled to run rapids that you do not think are within your ability or comfort level, especially on a

Take time to go over your plan before you launch on the river. Once you are paddling it can be hard to communicate.

Packrafts are light and portable, making them easy to portage around obstacles or through town. Here Forrest McCarthy carries his packraft through Mostar, Bosnia.

wilderness river trip where help is a long way away. Packrafts are easy to portage, even if you have to climb up and out of the river drainage to get around obstacles.

RIVER SIGNALS

Once you are moving downstream, verbal communication should be replaced with paddle or hand signals, since it is all too easy to misunderstand yells. If you are paddling with a group you've never been out with before, go over the signals before you hit the water so that everyone is on the same page. Most paddle signals are universal, but you may find regional variations, so take time to go over them with your group to ensure you are using the same ones.

Whistle

Boaters should carry a whistle attached to their PFD. Whistles are used to alert other members of your party in the event of an emergency. One

A whistle on your PFD is an important communication device for boaters. One blast is a call for attention; three or more blasts signal distress.

blast is a call for attention. Three blasts or repeated blasts are a call for help.

Whistles are used to signal others when someone flips or pins his or her boat and needs assistance.

In response to a whistle blast, paddlers should pull into an eddy to see what is happening and prepare to provide help if needed.

The sound of a whistle carries farther than a voice, but don't overestimate its power. If you are in a raging rapid, your whistle is unlikely to be louder than the noise of the river. So be sure you are always paying attention to your partners. Don't get too strung out on the river. Stay within eye contact with one another, and stop periodically to regroup and check in.

Paddle Signals

- Paddle straight up in the air: "Come down. OK to paddle," or "Run center."

- Paddle held horizontally up in the air, over the paddler's head: "Stop."

- Paddle held vertically and swung from side to side: Distress signal.

- Paddle held vertically and pointing either right or left at a 45-degree angle: "Paddle toward the direction the paddle is pointing" (e.g., if the paddle is pointed right, boaters head river right).

Hand Signals

- One finger held up and spun in a circle over the paddler's head: "Eddy out." Boaters should regroup in the same eddy.

- Pat top of head with one hand, point to someone: "Are you OK?" The signaler is asking if the person being pointed toward is OK. The person in question responds by patting his head if he is OK or by waving his arms if he is not. No response is taken to mean that the person is not OK.

- Thumbs up and pointing toward another boater: "Are you ready?" This signal asks if the boater is ready. The response is a thumbs-up.
- Point at eyes with two fingers and then in a direction: People should look in the direction the signaler indicates.

MOVING INTO THE CURRENT

Often you'll launch your boat from a beach or bank without much of an eddy, so you won't need to make an aggressive eddy turn to leave the shore and get into the main current of the river. You may be tempted to push off the bottom of the river with your paddle blade, and sometimes you have no choice. But prying and pushing with your blade can break it or wear down the edges. You are better off using your hands or making shallow paddle strokes into deeper water.

PADDLING

Any paddle stroke is better than none when you are in a rapid. Moving your blade through the water not only gives you momentum but also allows you to change direction and choose your path so that you, not the river, are in charge of where you are headed. Plus paddling adds stability, making you feel more balanced and secure in the water. If you just float downstream with your paddle in the air, you become a piece of flotsam subject to the whims of the current. In some situations this is fine, but most of the time you need to take control of where you are going to stay safe and make progress downstream. So keep paddling.

Remember to sink your whole blade into the water for maximum power and forward thrust.

BODY POSITION

We talked about your paddling position in chapter four, but when you start running whitewater, it's important to revisit the basics. To get into a strong paddling position, sit up straight with your legs out in front of you, feet pressed against the front of the boat and knees slightly bent and braced against your raft tubes. This position is your power position, but it has one weak link: your head and shoulders. Your head and shoulders weigh a lot. If they get thrown off to one side of your boat or the other, it

Make sure you are burying
your blade for maximum
power in each stroke.

is likely the rest of you will follow and you'll end up flipping unless you have a good, quick brace.

To help avoid capsizing, think loose hips. Your hips need to move up and down to absorb the impact of a churning river as it tosses you around. Don't let your shoulders follow that give-and-take. Rather think about a pivot point right around your belly button; below that point your hips are relaxed and fluid and constantly adjusting to changes by rising and falling. Above that pivot point, your upper body stays quiet and centered over the middle of the boat.

You will move your upper body forward and back at times to gain power or reach past a hole or turbulent wave. As long as you don't get pitched to one side, that backward and forward movement will enhance your power and absorb the shock of changing momentum or drops.

OPEN-BOAT PADDLING

Most of today's packrafts are either self-bailing or have tight-fitting spray skirts that keep water out of the boat. But sometimes you may get

To power through waves or holes, lean forward and paddle aggressively forward.

How to Sound Like a Pro—
Whitewater Terms

- **Bail,** verb: 1. To remove water from your boat; 2. To quit.
- **Boof,** verb: The act of running your boat off a drop.
- **Cfs (cubic feet per second),** noun: How many cubic feet of water pass through a given point per second. "The river was running 24,000 cfs."
- **Class,** noun: The difficulty rating of a whitewater rapid on a scale of I–VI.
- **Eddy,** noun: Area behind an obstacle where water flows in the opposite direction of the main current. Usually a good stopping point for boaters.
- **Eddy out,** verb: To pull into an eddy.
- **Gnarly,** adj.: A term used to describe something particularly difficult, scary, or really cool.
- **Gradient,** noun: Measurement of how steep a river is. Rivers with higher gradient tend to have bigger drops and more continuous rapids.
- **Peel out,** verb: To pull out of an eddy.
- **Permit,** noun: An official document allowing people to boat down a river. Permits are used to track users and limit numbers.
- **Portage,** verb: To walk around a rapid; noun: A specific spot where boaters carry or line their boats around an obstacle.
- **Put-in,** noun: The location where you put your boat into the water.
- **Rec level (recommended level),** noun: The water level best suited for boating a river.
- **Scout,** verb: Looking at a rapid before you run it.
- **Season,** noun: The time of year when a river is best for boating.
- **Shuttle,** noun: Arranging transportation between put-in and takeout so that you aren't stranded at the end of your trip.
- **Takeout,** noun: Where you take your boat out of the water at the end of your trip.

swamped if your spray skirt is off or you have an old-school spray deck that leaks. A boat full of water will feel sluggish and unresponsive, and will be difficult to maneuver.

To minimize the amount of water you ship into your boat when paddling without a spray deck, many packrafters back paddle through waves and riffles. Back paddling slows your boat down and helps prevent waves from breaking over the bow. Some boaters do not like back paddling, however, because you lose your forward momentum, making it hard to punch your boat through holes or waves.

In big water you need to be aggressive and use a strong forward stroke to propel your lightweight raft through the turbulence. For this reason, if you plan to run rapids, you should have some kind of covering on your packraft—or use a self-bailing boat—to help keep water out and allow you to push forward rather than backward through rapids.

WAVES

The original packrafts were shaped like miniature whitewater rafts: oval. These boats tended to flip over backward in big holes or waves, and the term "bandersnatch"—first coined by Cody Roman Dial—was born. This does not happen as much with the newer boats.

Today more and more packrafts sport a pointy, kayak-like shape. The advantage of the new shape is that the boat is more hydrodynamic for cutting through waves and has more volume in the stern to keep you from getting bandersnatched or popping a wheelie as you paddle down through standing waves. The advantage of the older design is that the rafts are usually lighter and more packable for backpacking.

A load on the bow can help counteract the backward force of a wave and help you stay upright regardless of the shape of your packraft. Most paddlers lean into their paddle strokes aggressively to prevent getting pushed back. You can also avoid big waves by looking for sneak routes around them. Often that just means riding along the edge of the wave train away from the crests. Watch out for eddy lines if you are off to the side of the main current. It can be easy to get pulled into an eddy unexpectedly if you aren't paying attention.

A load on the bow of your packraft can help flatten the boat and counter your weight in the stern so that you are less likely to get flipped backward in big waves. This was especially true in older-style packrafts without pointy ends.

Packrafts are small and have a shallow enough draft to allow you to sneak around some rapids by linking small side channels. If you don't like what you see downriver, get out of your raft, strap it on your back, and walk around any obstacle that causes you concern.

MANEUVERING IN RAPIDS

Packrafts spin—or pirouette—readily, enabling you to change direction with a flick of your paddle. On the flip side, they are slow and hard to power through strong currents because of their light weight, high profile, and shallow draft. Understanding the strengths and limitations of your boat will help you pick lines through rapids.

You can think of packrafters as inner tubers on a snow slope and hard-shell kayakers as slalom skiers. Packrafts are at their best making spinning turns and short accelerations but have no edge or ability to carve. They tend to bounce off obstacles and are hard to flip. Kayaks can

Newer-style packrafts have pointier ends like an inflatable kayak to help with stability.

be put up on edge to carve aggressively. They are faster and can power through waves and holes more easily than a packraft. They are also a lot tippier and harder to master.

As you head into a rapid, look where the current is flowing. That current is going to carry you where it wants if you do not place your boat on it with precision. Don't just let yourself get swept downstream, reacting to the obstacles as they confront you. Look for smooth channels, and place your boat on the current that is flowing in the direction you want to head. Aim and move where you want using powerful, effective strokes.

To help illustrate this idea, think about driving on the interstate. If you see an accident ahead of you, you change lanes to avoid it rather than drive at the obstruction as fast as you can. Likewise in a packraft, you want to choose the lanes or channels that avoid obstructions rather than try to power your way around or over them.

You've probably heard about using your eyes in sports. Skiers talk about looking at the space between trees. Mountain bikers focus their gaze up the trail rather than straight down. The principle behind using

Packrafts are like the inner tubers of the winter sports world, especially the old stubby models.

your eyes is that your body tends to follow them. That becomes problematic if you get fixated on the very thing you want to avoid, like a big hole or rock. Instead, focus on the spaces or channels where you want to move your boat. Look downstream so that you can plan your moves rather than just respond to the next obstacle.

Momentum

Moving forward with power allows you to drive your packraft across the surface of the water. You don't always have to be powering forward,

Your goal in a rapid is to place your boat on the current that is flowing in the direction you want to travel. This packrafter is on a green tongue of water, indicating a channel between obstacles in the river.

Momentum helps you punch through holes and waves.

however. Many packrafters spend a lot of time back paddling to slow their boats and assess what is going on downstream. But if you are running holes or through really big waves, you need momentum to power through.

Direction of Your Bow

You can go down rapids facing almost any direction, and all of us have been spun around backward at least once in our boating lives. It's good to be able to stay calm if your boat gets deflected off your desired course, but it's also important to go into a rapid with a plan that you intend to execute. Most plans have you pointing your bow in the direction you plan to travel. That enables you to power your boat away from the obstacles you want to avoid and onto the chutes or channels that will carry you safely through the whitewater.

To avoid bumping into obstacles like the side of a canyon, place your packraft on current moving away from the obstacle and angle your bow in the direction you want to travel—in this case, away from the canyon wall.

Beware: Pointing your bow in the direction you want to travel is just one part of the equation. You also need to place your boat on the current you want to be on, or be in a position that allows you to access that current if you find you don't like where you are heading. You can be pointed away from the obstacle you want to avoid, but if your boat is on the current running toward it, you are likely to get carried right into the obstacle despite the orientation of your boat.

Perhaps the best example of aiming your bow in your desired direction of travel is on a bending rapid. As we mentioned earlier, the outside of the bend is where most of the river's current will flow. Often the outside of the bend will also have steep banks, rocky outcrops, or strainers that you want to avoid. But it can be hard to avoid those obstacles if you are caught in the current with your bow pointing toward them. You might not have the strength you need to cross the main current to safety. Instead, enter the rapid with the nose of your boat pointing slightly to the inside of the bend. As you move downriver, paddle to the inside of the main current, pulling your boat away from any objective hazards on the outside.

Punching through Holes

You may not even notice it when you hit a small hole, but as holes draw in more water, their stopping power gets stronger and they become a significant obstacle for boaters. Remember, a hole is similar to an eddy. Water in a hole is flowing upstream, opposite the flow of the main current. When you hit a hole, that upstream flow can stop you in your tracks.

To punch through a hole effectively, you want to have speed. Paddle straight ahead hard, leaning forward to help you absorb the shock when your boat hits upstream flow. If you can, reach your paddle up and over the downstream side of the hole, grabbing into the main current and pulling your boat out the bottom end of the hole. Be prepared to brace in case the sudden deceleration of your boat that occurs when you enter the hole throws you off balance. Keep paddling forward until you broach the bottom of the hole, where you can get your blade into the green water outside the froth and take a deep stroke to pull you back into the main current.

To power over drops and through holes, paddle forward aggressively. Aim to plant your paddle over the edge of the drop or in the green water beyond a hole to pull yourself through the froth. Lean forward and paddle hard.

CHOOSE YOUR OBJECTIVE WISELY

Beginner boaters should increase the difficulty of the rivers they boat slowly. It's easy to get into trouble quickly on moving water and often hard to get out of it. The best bet when you first start out is to look for pool-drop rivers that give you a chance to regroup between rapids. A continuous flow of whitewater makes it hard to pull to the side if you need to scout and can mean a long swim if you come out of your boat. Or pick small, splashy Class II rivers for your first adventures.

Go with people who know the river and can coach you through the difficulties. It helps to have someone tell you where to go and what to do when your skills are still developing. It also helps to have someone watch you and give you tips on the things you are doing right and the things you could improve. Try not to get defensive. Sometimes it's hard to have

Water Levels

The character of a river changes dramatically with the water level. What can be a mellow run in low water can change into a frothy, churning maelstrom when the water comes up. Some rapids get harder at high levels; others get washed out and easier. Technical rapids can get more difficult when the levels drop and more rocks are exposed.

The main risk with high water is that eddies get washed out. When a river fills or overflows its banks, boaters are left with no escapes—no places where they can pause, regroup, and assess what is coming up downstream. If you come out of your boat and swim in these conditions, you may go for a very long way before you can get out of the water. In addition, you are more likely to encounter sweepers when rivers are at flood stage. This makes boating in floodwaters highly dangerous and appropriate only for experts.

At low water levels like pictured here, this river features lots of small eddies where a packrafter can get out of the main current. At high water this section of the river would be one continuous stretch of whitewater, making the consequences of a swim more dangerous.

When you first start packrafting, choose objectives with low potential consequences. Packrafting through cities and towns means you are closer to help if you need it.

someone critiquing your run when you are elated for having made it through in one piece and just want to bask in the glory of that accomplishment. In the long run, the feedback will make you a better boater, so suck it up and listen.

MENTAL PREPARATION

Whitewater boating can be exhilarating and terrifying. Fear is a natural reaction to being tossed and tumbled down a raging river in a little bouncy packraft. Plus fear can be a great motivator. It's a protective mechanism that sends a jolt of energy through our bodies so we are prepared for battle. That energy can be helpful on the river, but it can also be paralyzing. Some of us are good at facing our fears; some of us shut down instead. If you shut down in the middle of a rapid, that's a problem.

One of the best ways to combat fear on a river is to tackle objectives that are well within your comfort level and then slowly up the challenge as you gain confidence and experience. But you still may find yourself with sweaty palms and a racing heart at the top of every rapid. Here are a few mental tricks to help you harness your anxiety and use it as a source of power on your next boating excursion.

1. **Stop and look at where your fear is coming from.** Fear often stems from the unknown, a lack of control, feeling unsafe, or the anticipation of difficulty. The question is: Is that fear rational? If your answer is, "Yes, my fear is based on a real hazard," you need to decide if you are willing to take the risk and face the consequences of confronting that hazard. If your answer is no—that is, your fear is not rational—calm yourself down by verbalizing what could happen if you make a mistake. Usually you'll realize that not much could happen and that you are OK.

2. **Make sure you understand the consequences.** In whitewater boating you do face potentially life-threatening hazards, especially as you up the difficulty of the rivers you run. But in moderate or easy water, the main consequence you face is usually swimming. Swimming rapids can be scary, especially if you are carried a long distance. You can dif-

If you are new to whitewater, choose partners who can guide and support you as you learn.

fuse your fear of swimming by practicing it. Find a rapid with minimal consequences and a safe run-out, and take a swim. (Post spotters to help you if you need assistance, and wear a PFD and a helmet.) Once you've faced an unknown like swimming a rapid, you'll often find it's not as bad as you thought it would be and your fear level will drop.

3. **Paddle with people you trust and make you feel safe.** Your paddling partners are your support and your backup. It's important that you trust their skills and that you can communicate openly and honestly with one another. You should be able to admit you are scared and be supported by your colleagues. At times, peer pressure can be helpful in pushing us to test our limits, but we should always be comfortable stepping away from that when we don't feel right about the decisions being made.

4. **Break down the river.** You may find yourself fueled by anxiety for hours as you anticipate a big, challenging rapid that lies ahead. This anxiety affects your ability to enjoy your experience on the river and may have a negative impact on your performance as well. Prepare for the day by checking to see if you can scout and/or walk the rapids you

Be sure you trust your paddling partners before you head off on a wilderness trip with them.

will encounter. And remember, it's OK to walk. It's OK to look at a rapid. Knowing that you don't have to run everything can help you focus on what is immediately downstream so that you aren't wasting energy worrying about some unknown challenge miles ahead. Instead, take each rapid as it comes.

5. **Remove yourself from the action, and breathe to restore calm.** Sometimes you just need to pull over and get out of the flow of the river for a minute to relax and recharge. Breathe, look around, have a snack, and relax to help dissipate your anxiety.

6. **Find a mantra.** We all remember the "Little Engine That Could" chanting, "I think I can, I know I can, I know I can . . ." as it charged up the mountainside. Similarly, it helps to have some kind of phrase or song to focus on as you move through a rapid. Some people say, "Paddle, paddle, paddle," over and over; others recite Shakespeare. Anything that can help you quiet your mind and focus works.

7. **Have fun and enjoy the moment.** If you get too focused on the rapids, you tend to miss what's happening around you. Take time

to enjoy your surroundings and appreciate the beauty. Smile, laugh, and take pleasure in the experience. If you are frozen with fear all day long, you won't realize until you are off the river and heading home that you've been in a really amazing place with a great group of friends.

8. **Make sure you are comfortable.** Hunger, cold, fatigue, or body aches and pains can affect your ability to be in the present. If you are feeling uncomfortable, stop and fix the problem. You are much less likely to make bad decisions or mistakes when you are warm, dry, fed, and well rested.

DECIDING TO TURN AROUND

Fear can be irrational. It can lead you to be overly conservative and cautious. But there are times when you really are in danger—when you really should listen to that inner voice that is telling you to stop what you are doing.

Be sure to choose rivers that are within your comfort zone. Start with mellow objectives; as you gain skill and confidence, you can up the ante.

What Really Kills Boaters?

In most recreational boating accidents that result in fatalities, at least one of the following factors is present:

- Alcohol
- Absence of a PFD
- Flooded rivers
- Hypothermia

Removing these factors from your boating excursion reduces the likelihood of a bad outcome should someone come out of his or her boat.

Figuring out the difference between rational and irrational fears involves evaluating the consequences of your actions. A common way to do this is by the following equation:

Risk = Likelihood × Consequences

For example, if the desired action is to run a rapid, using this equation you'd consider how likely it is that you could flip and swim and what the consequence of flipping and swimming would be. Your risk is low if the rapid is easy and well within your ability so that the likelihood of a flip is minimal. Your risk is also low if a flip would just result in a short, unthreatening swim into a pool downstream. Your risk goes up if a swim would be dangerous or your likelihood of flipping is high.

The Risk = Likelihood × Consequences equation can help you separate the real danger you face from the dangers you are creating in your head.

But understanding the risk doesn't always translate into a good decision about moving forward. All groups face the possibility of succumbing to groupthink. Groupthink is what happens when no one in your party is willing to speak up and call it quits or question a decision. It can be hard to decide to stop, especially when you have committed time, money, and effort to the goal. All of us are susceptible to letting these factors color our decision.

Not all packrafters have the skill or desire to tackle difficult whitewater. Make sure you are comfortable with your group's goals and have accepted the consequences of your decision before you jump on a river that pushes your limits.

To help ensure you aren't being blinded by some unspoken agenda, ask yourself the following questions:

1. Does everyone feel safe and comfortable? As mentioned above, our physical well-being affects our ability to make sound decisions. If you are cold, hungry, or frightened, fix the problem before trying to decide if it's safe to continue downstream.

2. Are you feeling any outside pressure to achieve this goal? Be honest with yourself. This pressure could be subtle; you may not even be aware of its influence. Perhaps you want to enhance your status. Maybe you have dropped hundreds of dollars and taken time off from work to make the trip. If you can identify the pressure, you can decide if it is a legitimate reason to carry on.

3. What happens if you turn around? Sometimes going back involves a lot of hard work, and your reluctance to abort the trip reflects your unwillingness to tackle that physical challenge or deprivation again.

4. What happens if you continue forward? What is the risk of moving ahead? Could you die, or will you just be late or uncomfortable? It's important to honestly weigh the potential consequences of moving ahead against those of retreating.

5. What if you just don't know? Sometimes after you've asked yourself these questions, you still don't have a good answer. In these circumstances, it's important to listen to the most conservative voices in your party and to acknowledge bad feelings. Remember, surviving this trip means you can always try it again when things feel right.

CHAPTER SEVEN

HAZARDS AND BASIC RESCUE

BOATING IS FUN, BUT IT CAN BE DANGEROUS. MOVING WATER DOESN'T stop to give you a chance to regroup when things go wrong. You have to get yourself out of the current and into a safe spot before you can take a breath and calm down. For this reason, it is important to have an accurate understanding of your abilities and to pay attention to conditions as you descend so that you are not swept into a hazard unaware.

RISK

The main risk for boaters is drowning. If you are upright in your boat floating downstream, you can't drown. But if you end up in the river—or

As you push your packrafting skills, you are likely to come out of your boat and go for a swim. Be sure you know what to do to get yourself out of trouble. This packrafter is using his paddle to help pull himself back to his packraft.

Rescue Priorities

As in all emergency situations, you don't help anyone if you get in trouble trying to come to the rescue. The welfare of the rescuer always comes first, followed in descending order by that of the support team, the victim, and, last, the victim's equipment. That's not to say you don't try to help. It means that you don't make matters worse by getting into a dangerous predicament trying to provide assistance.

pinned upside down in your packraft—you can. Strainers, undercut rocks, holes, and big waves are some of the obvious hazards that pitch people out of their boats or pin them against an obstacle. Once you are in the water, you are vulnerable, especially in cold water, where hypothermia can quickly drain your energy, making swimming to safety hard or impossible. For all these reasons, it's important to be prepared for a flip and to have a plan for what to do if you find yourself swimming.

HAZARDS

River hazards include undercut rocks, strainers, and unrunnable white-water. Your best bet is to avoid these hazards. To do that, find out as much as you can about a river before you go. You don't want to find yourself tackling Class V whitewater when you are only comfortable in Class II. If you are on a wilderness river that doesn't have a lot of information written up about it, take time to scout ahead so that you can get off the river if there are dangerous hazards ahead.

Rolling a Packraft

Very few people ever learn to roll a packraft in the manner people roll kayaks, but it can be done, especially if your packraft is fitted with thigh straps. If you want to learn to roll a packraft, practice in a kayak first and then try to transfer the skill to your packraft.

Don't allow yourself to get swept into a rapid or around a blind curve without knowing what is below. Once you get pushed under a rock or caught up in a strainer, it can be very difficult if not impossible to get you out.

SWIMMING

As mentioned in chapter four, it's important to practice exiting and entering your packraft in moving water until you feel confident in your ability to do both. That said, there are going to be times when you cannot get back into your boat and are faced with swimming a rapid.

If you are unable to reenter your boat, try to hang onto both it and your paddle and swim. The defensive swimming position is to flip over onto your back, feet out in front of you, facing downstream. This position allows you to fend off rocks with your feet and protects your head and body from getting bashed up as the current carries you.

You may find you cannot hold onto both your boat and paddle due to the nature of your swim. If you can make a choice, your decision should

If you cannot get back into your boat after capsizing, try to hang onto it and your paddle and swim to the side of the river.

If you come out of your packraft and find yourself floating downriver, flip over onto your back with your feet pointed downstream. This defensive position protects your head and allows you to push off obstacles with your feet.

be dictated by your situation. On a wilderness trip where your gear is critical to your safety, you should try to hold onto your boat. If you are closer to the road, it may be better to hold onto your paddle, since it is harder to keep track of a paddle than a packraft. If at any time you feel as though your gear is jeopardizing your safety, let go of it and take care of yourself.

Keep looking for eddies on the side of the river. If you see one, flip over onto your belly and swim as hard as you can toward it. It can be hard to swim with your raft. If you are running a pool-drop river, your best bet may be to go all the way through the rapid with your boat until you reach the pool below and then swim to shore in the calm water. If the river rapids are more continuous, you may need to let go of your boat to get to shore. Hopefully you are not paddling alone, and another member of your party is available to rescue the boat.

Don't stand up until you are in ankle-deep, calm water. Instead, pull yourself to shore using your hands.

As you are carried downstream, look for eddies where you can get out of the main current. If you see one, flip over onto your stomach and swim hard toward it.

TOWING A SWIMMER IN WITH YOUR PACKRAFT

In bigger rapids, it helps to post spotters sitting in their packrafts in eddies throughout the whitewater. These spotters can come to the rescue if another member of their party flips and needs assistance. Kayakers often wear a tow system around their waist (you can buy one from most boating stores) that they use to pull a swimmer to shore, and boaters who routinely paddle Class IV water or above often wear rescue vests that include a built-in quick-release harness system for towing.

You can create your own tow system with an 8- to 10-foot piece of webbing. Attach the webbing to your waist with a quick-release buckle. If something happens, you can release the tow system by unclipping the buckle and paddling away from the rope.

The excess webbing can be stuffed loosely into a stuff sack and clipped onto your belt with a carabiner. If someone needs your help, you can toss the bag to him. He should grab onto the line (not the bag) with both hands, flip onto his back with the rope riding over one shoulder, and

Foot Entrapment

It's hard to see what is under the surface of the river. Rocks, logs, and other obstacles may be hidden by frothy or murky water. These things can easily trap a foot. When this happens in moving water, you are in trouble. The water pushes you down, forcing your head underwater while your foot remains pinned upstream. Foot entrapment can easily lead to drowning. A life jacket is unlikely to help, as the force of the water pushing down on the swimmer's back usually overwhelms the flotation in the vest.

Rescuing someone whose foot is trapped in moving water is very difficult and rarely successful. Sometimes you can run a rope across the river and under the victim's armpits to help hold up his or her head and buy yourself some time to come up with a plan. In some situations, rescuers can wade to the person to provide assistance, but this is an advanced rescue technique. Remember that the first rule of first aid is the safety of the rescuer. If one person's foot got stuck when he or she tried to stand up in the current, it's very likely yours could too.

The best way to minimize the risk of foot entrapment is to never stand up or put your feet down unless the water depth is below your knees or the water is calm. Don't panic if you come out of your boat. Float downriver on your back until you can swim to the side of the river or another boater rescues you.

hang on while you paddle him to shore. If your swimmer has the energy, have him kick to assist you as you paddle.

If you want to forgo the added weight of a dedicated tow system, tie a piece of webbing between the stern tie-downs to create a handle for swimmers to hold onto. They can use the handle to pull their torso up onto the stern of the packraft and out of the water and can kick aggressively to help the paddler move the boat forward.

THROW ROPES FROM SHORE

Often the best way to reach a swimmer is to throw a rope from shore, but this is a tricky skill to master. Throw bags don't feel or act the way a

Have swimmers grab onto the stern of your packraft (having a grab line to hold onto can help) to tow them to shore. It helps if swimmers kick.

ball does when you throw it; plus you have the current to contend with in your aim and often have only one shot to reach the victim before he is carried away downstream. Take time to practice tossing your throw bag along moving water to develop your accuracy and range.

Rescuer

In the best-case scenario, you have spotters posted along the sides of a rapid armed with their throw bags and ready to be of assistance if someone takes a swim. Choose your location as a spotter carefully. You need to be in a secure, balanced position where you can brace yourself against the weight of the swimmer. Find a spot with slow water or an eddy downstream that will serve as a safe landing zone for your victim.

If you are not already in position when your partner flips, you'll have to run to a good spot to make a toss.

When you get in position, yell or blow your whistle to alert the swimmer to your presence and the fact that you are there to throw a rope

If you are running a rapid where it is likely someone in your group might swim, it's a good idea to post spotters with throw ropes ready to provide assistance if necessary.

to him if needed. If you can't get the swimmer's attention, don't throw the rope.

Try to throw the bag when the swimmer is straight across from you or slightly upstream so that you create an angle when he weights the rope that will allow him to pendulum into shore.

Get into an athletic stance, with your front foot braced. You may also choose to sit down after you throw the bag so that you are in a stronger position to withstand the force of the swimmer and the current.

You can throw the bag overhand, underhand, or sidearm. All work. In general, overhand and sidearm throws have more distance. Underhand throws tend to be more accurate and are good for short, quick tosses. Place the bag in your throwing hand and the end of the rope in the other hand. Pull out a couple of arm lengths of rope before you toss so that you have room to wind up for a big throw. Aim to hit the swimmer in the head with the bag. Remember to keep hold of the end of the rope and remove any carabiners you may have used to clip the throw bag to your packraft.

When the swimmer grabs the rope, try to pull out any slack in the system and brace yourself for the impact of his weight. If the force feels too powerful, sit down or walk down the shore to reduce the pressure on the rope. If you are having a hard time holding on, the swimmer probably is too. You can flip the rope behind your back and hip belay him to shore using friction from the rope running across your body to help you resist the force of the river. You can also get your teammates to grab onto your PFD to help hold you in place.

Don't wrap the rope around your hands or arms for better purchase. The rope can quickly change from an aid to a deadly trap if you get entangled in it and pulled into the river.

Swimmer

If you find yourself swimming, be alert and on the lookout for a rescuer as you get carried downstream. When the rope lands, try as hard as you can to get to it. Grab the rope—not the bag, as there may be more line

Once the throw rope is deployed, brace yourself for the impact of the swimmer's weight. If you have more than one person on shore, they can help hold you in place, or you can brace yourself against a rock. Hold the rope around your back for added friction.

Swimmers should place the throw rope over their outside or upstream shoulder and flip over onto their back, kicking hard to help the rescuers. This swimmer will pivot downstream and into shore as the rope gets taut.

in the bag—with both hands and hang on tight. You'll feel a strong jerk when the slack goes out of the system and the rope goes taut. Be ready for that pull. Flip over onto your back and place the rope over your outside shoulder (the one facing away from the shore and your rescuer). It's easier to keep your head above water in this position, plus placing the rope on the outside facilitates your pendulum swing into shore. Kick hard to help your rescuers pull you.

PINNED RAFTS OR SWIMMERS

Packrafts are harder to pin than other crafts. They are small and tend to bounce off obstacles. You can often dislodge them by rocking your body around and pushing away from rocks with your hands. But you can pin a packraft, especially in big water or if you get swept into vegetation on the outside of a bend, where the force of the current is holding you and your boat in place.

In general, the first thing to do to try to unpin your packraft is to let out some air. Sometimes this is enough to allow you to move it out of the force of the current and off the obstacle. Try to work with the forces of the river. Look at the situation. Play with angles. Your goal is to use lateral forces to shift the angle of the boat so that the current moves it off the obstacle. You don't want to try to pull a packraft upstream, fighting the current. Rather, use your team to haul on a rope tied to the raft in a way that swings one end into the current and off the obstacle that pins it.

Attach your throw rope to the grab loop on either the bow or stern of the raft (depending on the direction you want to shift the boat to get it off the obstacle) using a lightweight locking carabiner. Get your team together to help pull on the rope. The more people, the easier the work.

To avoid accidental entanglement, make sure no one wraps the rope around a hand. In addition, make sure you don't have a lot of slack rope lying around that could snare someone's foot.

Pull downstream with the current.

If you are unable to remove the packraft using the power of your team, you may need to set up a 3-to-1 pulley system. Pulley systems work best with throw ropes made from Spectra. Polypropylene is often not strong enough to withstand the forces of a pulley system. In general, you should only expect to encounter conditions where you need to use a pulley system in powerful rivers with a lot of current.

3-to-1 Pulley

To build a 3-to-1-pulley system, start by anchoring your rope to a large tree or boulder. Use a bowline knot to secure the line. Next clip a bend in the rope to the pinned packraft with a carabiner. Choose your attachment point to minimize the amount you have to pull against the current.

For a simple 3-to-1, make a loop in the rope near the anchor point by tying an overhand on a bight. This knot will get really tight once you start pulling on the rope, so you may want to place a stick or carabiner in it that you can remove when you are done to give you enough slack to get the knot out. Clip a second carabiner into the loop, and run your rope through the carabiner. You can now get your team to pull on the rope, using the mechanical advantage of the pulley system to give you added power.

This simple system has some disadvantages. It is not adjustable, and your team will be pulling toward the river, which means you could run out of room before you get the packraft unpinned. But it's quick and easy, and if you just need a little extra help, it can be enough.

For more information on rescue pulley systems, take a swiftwater rescue course or search online for instructional videos.

TEAMWORK

Rescue and first-aid situations are one place where peer leadership is not very effective. You often need to take quick, decisive action and don't have time to consult all members of your team to get their opinions. In an emergency, someone needs to step forward and take on the leadership role. That individual can designate jobs to other members of the team as the rescue unfolds.

It helps for the team leader to stay out of the action if possible. That way he or she can keep tabs on what is happening and respond to

In an emergency, it is important to use all your resources to help one another and to have a leader who can oversee what is going on and provide guidance and a plan.

perceived needs. If you don't have enough people for this scenario, make sure the leader steps back occasionally to consider the big picture. Don't let yourself get sucked into tying the perfect knot when your role is to oversee the entire setup.

When devising a rescue plan, make sure it is simple, clean, and efficient. You often don't have time to shift gears mid-rescue, so make sure you have a workable solution before you commit to it. This is where swift-water rescue training and practice are invaluable. You want to be able to respond quickly and efficiently in an emergency, which means you need to know what you are doing *before* you get into trouble.

Once the crisis passes, you can ease back on the directive leadership and bring your team in to help make decisions. Play it by ear. You'll know when it's OK to slow down and allow some conversation about what to do next.

CHAPTER EIGHT

FIRST AID

IF YOU PLAN TO SPEND A LOT OF TIME IN THE WILDERNESS, YOU SHOULD take a wilderness first-aid course and cardiopulmonary resuscitation (CPR). Wilderness first aid is different from the basics you learn in the city, where an ambulance is usually just a few minutes away. In the wilderness it can take hours, if not days, for you to get help, so you need to know how to stabilize and care for an injured or sick person for a long time.

This is not a first-aid book; however, there are some river-specific health and safety concerns that are worth mentioning.

COLD-WATER SWIM

Most of the time, an unexpected flip and swim is relatively inconsequential. Sure it can be startling and even scary, but it's usually not hard to get back into your packraft. Flipping your boat happens when you push your boating skills and tackle more difficult objectives. It's the way you get better, and if you are wearing the right clothes for a swim, you'll be fine. So don't panic if you come out of your boat.

However, you don't want to underestimate the dangers of swimming in rapids—especially cold-water rapids. Swimmers can get chilled and exhausted quickly if they are in the river for a long time. The rule of thumb for unprotected cold-water immersion is 1-10-1. One minute of cold-water shock, during which your breathing and heart rate accelerates. Ten minutes of functional movement, when you have the physical power and strength to fight to help yourself. And 1 hour before you pass out

In the Arctic any swim is risky because of the temperature of the water. Dress warmly to help prevent hypothermia.

from hypothermia if you remain submerged. Obviously these times are extended if you are wearing proper attire such as a dry suit. But it's still important to recognize that people get cold fast.

If a member of your party swims, your first step is to get him or her out of the water. The individual's condition determines your next step. Most of the time he or she will be just fine. But you do need to be prepared to administer first aid if the swimmer is cold or injured.

Do a quick patient assessment to determine the swimmer's condition. This includes the ABCDEs of first aid (airway, breathing, circulation, disability, and environment). If your patient's ABCs are compromised—say she isn't breathing or is bleeding profusely—you need to stop and treat that problem right away. These are life-threatening problems, and your patient will die if you don't address them.

PATIENT EXAM

Once you've gone over the initial ABCs, you may want to conduct a head-to-toe exam. If your patient bumped down through rocks at high speed, the mechanism for injury is real, and you want to be sure your

Threats to Life, the ABCDEs

Here are a few simple things you can do in the first 5 minutes after an accident to save someone's life:

- **Airway:** People die quickly if they do not have an airway or an open passage to get oxygen into their lungs. If someone is drowning, get him or her to shore and immediately check to see if the airway is open. If your patient can talk, she has an airway, is breathing, and has a pulse. That means you can move on to see if she is bleeding or is suffering some traumatic injury. If your patient is unconscious and you cannot detect breathing, tilt her head back and lift her chin. Often this will be enough to restore breathing.
- **Breathing:** Look, listen, and feel for signs of breathing. Is her chest rising and falling, can you feel air against your cheek, or can you hear breath sounds? If you do not detect any signs of breathing after 20 seconds or so, maintain your patient's head tilt and blow two quick breaths into her mouth. If the breaths go in, continue rescue breathing at a rate of about 20 breaths per minute. If the breaths do not go in, reposition the head and try again. If you still cannot get air in, look in the person's mouth to see if there is anything obstructing the airway. If there is, remove it; if there isn't, reposition the head with the head-tilt, chin-lift technique and try again to blow air into the lungs. Keep

patient has no other problems, such as a head or neck injury or a broken bone. If you know the patient was in the water for a long time and has gotten cold, you can skip this step.

Take a few minutes to ask the patient a few basic questions. You can get a good sense of a person's level of consciousness by asking his name, where he is, what day and time it is, and what happened. If your patient has trouble answering these questions, be on the lookout for further deterioration and consider the possibility of a head injury.

Any threat to life is serious. If you are deep in the wilderness, it can take a long time to get your patient to a hospital, especially if he cannot trying until you succeed or someone with more experience and training takes over.

- **Circulation:** If you are trained in CPR, once you establish breathing—either because the patient is breathing on her own or you are doing rescue breathing—check for a pulse and go into the CPR routine. If you are not trained, continue rescue breathing if necessary and check for bleeding by sweeping your hands all over your patient's body to look for blood. If your patient is wearing a dry suit, you will need to get inside the suit to detect bleeding, as blood will not pass through the waterproof material. If you find major hemorrhaging, try to control the bleeding by placing a sterile dressing—or whatever you have that can absorb the blood—directly onto the wound and pressing down. Elevate the area above the heart if possible.

- **Disability:** Check quickly for any obvious signs of trauma. Consider the mechanism of injury. If your patient has taken a big swim through a rocky rapid, have her lie quietly and keep her head or neck still until you can ensure that she has not sustained a head or neck injury. You can immobilize your patient by having someone place a hand on her head or by placing bags around it to help remind her not to move.

- **Environment:** Remember, it's likely your patient is going to be cold. Get her out of the water and into a warm, dry place. Have her lie on a pad or something to insulate her from the ground. Stabilize your patient as best you can, and seek help.

walk or boat. Monitor the individual's vital signs (pulse, respiration rate, level of consciousness, skin color and temperature, and pupil size and evenness) every 30 minutes or so (more if you suspect a serious injury) to keep track of his condition. A normal adult has a resting pulse between 60 and 80 beats per minute; breathes 12 to 20 times per minute; has pink, warm, dry skin (in dark-skinned people, look at nail beds to detect skin color); and has pupils that are even in size and reactive to light. A normal level of responsiveness is a person who can say her name, location, time, and what happened. Any indication of deterioration in these vital signs ups the urgency of the evacuation.

It is helpful to carry pain medication with you on wilderness expeditions. Recent research indicates that a maximum recommended dosage of ibuprofen taken in conjunction with the maximum recommended dosage of acetaminophen can provide as much pain relief as prescription pain medications. You can take the ibuprofen and acetaminophen together or, better yet, stagger the two every 4 hours.

SIGNS AND SYMPTOMS OF HYPOTHERMIA

Hypothermia—or too little heat—causes a gradual deterioration in a patient's mental and physical abilities. At the far end of the spectrum, severely hypothermic patients are unresponsive. Severe hypothermia is deadly, so it's important to recognize what's happening and take action to stop it immediately. Your patient—or you—doesn't have to take a swim to be hypothermic. It can happen boating in cold, wet conditions. So be prepared.

As your core temperature begins to drop, you begin to get clumsy. At first it may be just your fine motor skills that are compromised. Your fingers don't work, and you can't zip up your jacket, for instance. If you get colder, your gross motor skills begin to be affected, and you may find yourself stumbling when you try to walk. Hypothermic patients often become apathetic or grumpy. Speech may be altered. As you slide from mild into moderate hypothermia, your level of consciousness deteriorates and you may answer questions inappropriately or be confused. The end of the spectrum is loss of consciousness.

It is often easier to detect signs of hypothermia in someone other than yourself. Keep an eye on one another when you are paddling in wet, cold conditions. Boaters say 50°F and rainy is prime hypothermia weather if you are unprepared, so pay attention if you are out in those conditions. And pay attention to swimmers; they get cold much faster.

Our bodies lose heat in a number of ways, one of which is convection, or the loss of heat to water or air moving past our skin. The rate of convective heat loss depends on the difference in temperature between your body and the water, but it can be as much as 25 times as chilling as standing in still, warm air. Remember this when you launch on a glacial river.

Treatment for Mild to Moderate Hypothermia

It is pretty easy to warm up when you first detect signs that you are getting too cold. Get out of the offending environment. Change into dry clothes, or seek shelter. Do some jumping jacks, run around, or swing your arms and legs. Exercise ups our heat generation 15 to 18 times, so if you feel chilled, moving will help warm you up.

As you get colder, you'll grow more apathetic and may just feel like curling up in a ball. Exercise can still help, but most likely you'll need someone to force you to move. As a caregiver, you may have to be more assertive in your treatment if your patient is becoming lethargic. Again, make sure the patient is in warm, dry clothes and out of the offending elements. Pull out your stove and heat up some water for a hot drink if the individual is able to drink from a cup without assistance.

You may want to light a fire. Some people carry an emergency reflective blanket in their packs for hypothermia treatment. If you have a fire, your patient can sit in front of it wearing the emergency blanket like a cape to trap the fire's radiant heat and help warm up.

If your patient is not responding to these treatments, it's time to get more aggressive. If you are on a wilderness trip, you'll have camping gear along so you can make a hypothermic wrap to warm your patient. To make a wrap, place a ground cloth or a tent fly on the ground. Lay a sleeping pad in the middle of the tarp kitty-corner to the midline. Place a sleeping bag on top of the pad.

Meanwhile, heat up a couple of liters of water on a stove or fire. The water does not have to boil; you just want it to be hot enough to warm—not burn—your patient. Pour the water into two or three water bottles. If it feels too hot to be next to your skin, wrap the bottle in a sock or T-shirt.

Have your patient strip down to his base layer and a warm hat and get into the sleeping bag. You will probably need to provide assistance.

Place the water bottles in the bag with him. It's nice to have the bottles near the patient's core: between the legs in the groin area or under the armpits. Zip up the sleeping bag and snug it tightly around your patient's head, leaving his face clear. Next fold the corner of the tarp by the patient's feet in over the sleeping bag, and then bring the sides of the tarp across him, tucking them in tightly. Wrap the tarp around the patient's head. Don't cover his face. Your patient will be swaddled in the tarp and should look like a burrito when you are done.

Our bodies warm slowly. If we get really cold, it could take hours to rewarm. During that time you'll need to replace the hot water bottles periodically. People who are less cold will recover more rapidly. Moderately hypothermic people are wiped out by the experience. If your patient takes hours to rewarm, he may take days to feel normal. In this scenario, you are not going to be able to get back in your boat and paddle immediately.

If your patient is severely hypothermic, gently wrap him up in a hypothermic wrap. Take care not to be too jarring or rough in your handling, as sudden movements can cause heart problems in a severely cold human. Place hot water bottles in with the patient, but be extra careful that the bottles are not too hot. These patients will be unable to tell you if they are getting burned. The hypothermic wrap will not rewarm the patient, but it can help prevent further heat loss. Go for help. This individual will need medical attention, but even if he appears dead, there is hope. Some severely hypothermic people have been successfully rewarmed.

Ultimately, hypothermia is preventable if you pay attention to the environmental conditions and respond quickly when you see signs and symptoms of someone getting too cold. Aim to stop the problem when you can still do jumping jacks to get warm.

DROWNING

Drowning or near drowning causes complex physiological responses. As a first responder, the details of what is going on are less important than the steps you can take to help save your patient.

One of the first things to be aware of is that drowning people do not always present in the thrashing, yelling, splashing way we expect after watching too many movies. People who are drowning are often exhausted and can barely stay above the water. All their energy goes into trying to get a breath, not yelling for help. It's important to keep your eyes on your packrafting partners if they go for a swim and try to get to them as quickly as possible.

This passivity changes if you get in the water next to someone who is drowning. Victims often panic and try to climb on top of rescuers in an attempt to get to the surface and air. You are better off approaching a drowning person with some kind of flotation device or a throw rope rather than your own body. Sometimes that is impossible, and advanced swiftwater rescue courses will teach you how to dive in and swim to the assistance of victims. But this technique is not without risks, and rescuers are usually connected to shore with a rope to help pull them back to safety. If you are planning to boat highly technical rivers, gaining this skill is imperative. If you are in more moderate water, you are better off focusing on using a throw rope or your boat to assist a swimmer.

If you pull an unresponsive victim out of the river, go immediately into your ABCs. CPR and rescue breathing can be effective in near-drowning situations. Be prepared for your patient to vomit up ingested water. Call for help.

OTHER RIVER AILMENTS

Trench Foot

Trench—or immersion—foot is nerve damage caused by prolonged exposure to cold, wet conditions. Trench foot is a nonfreezing injury that is most common in places like the Arctic or during early-season travel, when temperatures are cool and the weather wet.

Trench foot can be extremely painful, and most sufferers cannot walk. Treatment is rest and pain medication, but it's unlikely that the kind of pain meds most of us carry in our first-aid kits will relieve the pain your victim will experience. Only heavy-duty meds can dull the pain of acute immersion foot; most victims need to be evacuated.

To avoid trench foot, avoid cold feet. Wearing neoprene socks, Gore-Tex socks, or booties on the river can help. Dry suits with built-in socks are even better because your feet will not be wet during the day. If you feel your feet getting numb, stop and warm them up. Change your socks. Warm your feet on someone's belly. Swing your legs. Get out of your boat and run around. Avoiding trench foot is the best medicine.

Hand and Foot Cracks

If your hands and feet are wet all the time, you may end up with painful cracks in your skin. To help prevent cracking, wear socks and gloves, especially when you sleep at night. Slather your hands and feet with a thick cream: Bag Balm, Vaseline, and Eucerin all work well to help keep them moist.

On desert rivers, it's not uncommon to develop raw spots where the grit from silty water gets into your shoes and rubs away the skin. You can help prevent rubbing by wearing socks—even with sandals—and making sure your feet are dry and clean at night when you are sitting around camp.

Sunburn, Sun Bumps, and Cold Sores

Being on the water intensifies the power of the sun, making you more susceptible to burns. Intense UV exposure also can cause sun bumps, an itchy rash on the back of your hands and cheeks, and trigger the development of cold sores on your lips. As a boater you just want to be aware and take precautions, including wearing adequate sunscreen, a sunhat, and maybe even gloves to protect your skin. (Lightweight gardening gloves work well in hot weather; neoprene gloves are best when it's cold.)

Personal Hygiene

Sitting in a wet boat can get a little funky if you do it day in and day out and are wearing a wet suit or clammy dry suit. And hiking without taking a shower for days on end makes it hard to stay fresh as a daisy. It's important to take care of your nether parts when you are in the backcountry, and the best way to do that is to keep clean. Lots of backpackers carry a bandana dedicated to sponge baths; they clean off every day or so to ensure they don't end up with something itchy or painful.

To take a sponge bath, grab a dromedary or water jug and fill it with river water. Find a private spot 200 feet from shore and give yourself a good cleaning. If you use soap, make sure you rinse thoroughly, as soap residue can irritate your skin. Let yourself dry completely. The key is to not let things get too damp and warm down there. That's when you run into trouble.

Special River Regs

Most multiday rivers in the United States require some kind of permit to run. This is a reflection of the number of people who use these river corridors every year. Regulations on permitted rivers are often different than standard Leave No Trace techniques for the wilderness. So if you are packrafting on a permitted river, remember to follow the regulations, which may mean taking your sponge bath in the river instead of onshore, pouring strained dishwater right into the main current, and urinating directly into the water as well. The thinking behind these practices is the old adage that dilution is the best solution to pollution. Make sure you know how land managers want you to deal with wastewater and urine before you head out on your trip.

If you plan to spend a lot of time in challenging whitewater, take a swiftwater rescue course so that you have the tools you need to help someone—or yourself—if you get in trouble in a rapid.

FURTHER EDUCATION

Wilderness trips take you far from emergency care. You are on your own out there. That solitude is what makes expeditioning exciting, but don't be reckless in your adventuring. There's a difference between a skilled backcountry traveler attempting difficult challenges and a novice getting in over his or her head. Be realistic about your skills and experience, and choose objectives conservatively. You are responsible for the health and safety of yourself and your teammates. If you plan to partake in a wilderness packrafting trip, consider taking first-aid, CPR, and swiftwater rescue courses before you go. These courses will give you the tools you need to handle emergencies, improvise treatment, and get yourself out of trouble.

Some swiftwater rescue course providers are now offering courses that are specifically designed for packrafters. Look online to find courses near you.

CHAPTER NINE

LEAVE NO TRACE

WILDERNESS TRAVEL COMES WITH RESPONSIBILITY. THE THINGS THAT make it special—untrammeled nature, wildlife, clean air and water, flowers, trees, and scenic splendor—require respect and care to protect them for future generations.

The Leave No Trace Center for Outdoor Ethics has created seven general principles that guide backcountry travelers on how to move through the wilderness without causing harm to the land, water, and wildlife. These principles are meant to be guidelines that can be adapted to different circumstances and environments. They are not hard-and-fast rules, but rather suggestions that can help you travel lightly on the land that you love.

Many permitted rivers have additional requirements to help minimize impacts along the river corridor. These regulations make a lot of sense when you think about the fact that hundreds if not thousands of boaters are using the same campsites over and over again. Without special care, those sites would soon be trashed and unusable.

Packrafters should be aware of river and backcountry principles to help minimize their impact.

PLAN AHEAD AND PREPARE

- Know the regulations and special concerns for the area you'll visit.
- Prepare for extreme weather, hazards, and emergencies by carrying the proper gear and obtaining the required skills so you aren't forced to compromise your LNT ethics to ensure your safety.

Rivers can be great places to leave no trace—beaches and gravel bars change frequently, and your imprint is erased quickly. Try to stick to non-vegetated areas to minimize your impact.

- Schedule your trips to avoid times of high use.
- Visit in small groups when possible.
- Repackage food and plan meals carefully to minimize waste.
- Use a map, compass, and global positioning system (GPS) device to eliminate the use of marking paint, rock cairns, and flagging.

TRAVEL AND CAMP ON DURABLE SURFACES

- Durable surfaces include established trails and campsites, rock, gravel, dry grasses, snow, and rivers.
- Protect riparian areas by camping at least 200 feet from water, unless you are camping on rivers. Along most river corridors, the lowest-impact sites are established campsites on beaches or gravel bars along the water's edge.
- Good campsites are found, not made. Altering a site is not acceptable or necessary.

Rock makes an ideal traveling surface when you are trying not to leave any sign of your passing.

- In popular areas, concentrate use on existing campsites and keep campsites small, walk single file in the middle of the trail, and focus activity in areas where vegetation is absent.
- In pristine areas, disperse use to prevent the creation of new campsites and trails, move camp frequently, and avoid places where impacts are just beginning.

DISPOSE OF WASTE PROPERLY

- Pack it in, pack it out. Inspect your campsite and rest areas for trash or spilled foods. Pack out all trash, leftover food, and litter. Food scraps attract animals to campsites. Along river corridors where sites are heavily used, this creates problem animals, so keep a clean camp.
- Deposit human waste appropriately. In most wilderness areas, this means digging a cathole approximately 6 to 8 inches deep and at least 200 feet from water, campsites, and trails. In some heavily used areas, and along most regulated river corridors, you must

Camping on surfaces that show no signs of your passing, like sand or rock, will help minimize your impact on the land.

In southeastern Utah it's not uncommon to find pieces of pottery and other Native American artifacts. Leave the objects where you find them so that others can enjoy the excitement of discovery.

pack out all human waste. For packrafters, the best option is to carry some kind of portable sanitation system, such as WAG Bags or RESTOP bags. Some river management plans require your WAG Bag or RESTOP bags to be carried in a dry bag or hard-shell container. Packrafters have found that old plastic peanut butter jars work well for this purpose; they are lightweight and secure. Check with land managers to make sure your plan for dealing with solid waste meets their requirements.

MINIMIZE CAMPFIRE IMPACTS

- Campfires can cause lasting damage to the backcountry if they are used improperly. Use fires with care and only in areas where they are allowed and wood is plentiful.
- On most permitted rivers, users are required to carry a fire pan for their campfires. Packrafters can use an aluminum roasting pan as

a pan for campfires. To keep the aluminum from melting, place an inch of sand on the bottom of the roasting pan and then place the pan on top of rocks to avoid scorching the ground. When you are done with your fire, you can toss the sand into the river.

- Away from a regulated river, build fires in established fire rings, in fire pans, or on mineral soil on a beach or gravel bar.
- Burn all wood and coals to ash, put out campfires completely, and then scatter the cool ashes. On regulated rivers, you will need to pack out all your ashes.

RESPECT WILDLIFE

- Observe wildlife from a distance. Do not follow or approach animals. Be aware of the fact that you travel quickly and silently in a packraft and can come upon animals unexpectedly. Try to make noise to warn them of your approach. If you are causing animals distress, pull over and let them get away from you.
- Never feed animals. Feeding animals damages their health, alters natural behaviors, and exposes them to predators and other dangers.
- Control pets at all times or leave them at home.
- Avoid wildlife during sensitive times: mating, nesting, raising young, or winter.

BE CONSIDERATE OF OTHER VISITORS

- Respect other visitors and protect the quality of their experience.
- Be courteous. Yield to other users on the trail or on the river.
- Step to the downhill side of the trail when encountering pack stock.
- Take breaks away from trails and other visitors.
- Let nature's sounds prevail.
- When floating on rivers, don't pull in to a beach where another party is taking a break or camping unless you have no choice or are visiting a special site. Some rivers have assigned campsites;

on others the campsites are first come, first served. If you want to stop at a specific spot for the night, get moving early in the day to increase your chances of getting there before someone else does.

- As a packrafter, you are an ambassador for the sport. Packrafting has a long and rich history, but many view it as a new activity and are wary of its impact. Leaving a positive impression on other backcountry users by being respectful and courteous and minimizing your environmental impact is important to the future of our sport.

—ADAPTED FROM LNT.ORG

SPECIAL CONSIDERATIONS FOR PACKRAFTING IN GRIZZLY COUNTRY

Some of the best packrafting in the world takes place in grizzly bear country. It can be very easy to surprise a grizzly in your packraft. You move quickly and silently and may come around the corner and stumble upon a bear with no forewarning. Usually the bear will hightail it out of there, but in certain circumstances you may arouse a bear's aggressive tendencies and find yourself in trouble.

You need to follow a few special guidelines to ensure your safety as well as the animal's when you hike and boat in bear country. All too many grizzly bears end up dead after a chance encounter with humans. Most grizzlies don't want anything to do with people. But if you stumble upon one in the midst of a meal, protecting her young, or simply by surprise, the bear's natural reaction will be to protect itself, its food, or its young. Unfortunately, if there are too many of these encounters, game managers end up "removing" the bear—a euphemism for killing it. To avoid this, we need to be thoughtful when traveling in bear country.

Make noise—the number-one strategy for avoiding an unexpected encounter with a grizzly bear. This is true on the river as well as on the trail. You need to yell, especially if you are floating down a noisy, splashy creek. And you need to yell often so that any bears in the vicinity have plenty of time to catch the sound and decide if it's best to skedaddle. Bells have not been shown to be as effective as the human voice. So talk, sing, or babble while you walk and boat in bear country.

Some of the best packrafting spots in the world are in grizzly bear country. It's important to follow proper bear-camping procedures in these places to protect yourself and the bears.

Travel in groups—and by groups we mean three or more people close together. If you get spread out, the impact of your group is lost. So stay close when hiking or boating in grizzly bear country where you have limited visibility.

Carry bear spray. Bear spray has been proven to be the most effective way to avoid a bear attack. But you need to have your spray handy. Bear spray stuffed in the top of your pack or the dry bag on the deck of your packraft does you no good whatsoever if a bear starts to charge you. Every member of your party should carry bear spray, preferably in a holster, and have practiced pulling it out and shooting it off quickly so that they'll be able to use it if they need it.

Make yourself bigger. The recommended behavior in the face of a bear is to group up or open your jacket wide or raise your arms so that you look big. Talk quietly so the bear gets a sense of what you are. Pull out your bear spray. If the bear approaches, you want to deploy the bear spray when the animal is roughly 25 to 30 feet away. Beware of the wind direction. If the wind is coming toward you, wait longer.

If bear spray does not cause the bear to turn and run, drop to the ground and play dead, curling up under your backpack and protecting your neck and head with your hands. In many cases bears will lose interest if they no longer perceive you as a threat. Needless to say, playing dead, holding your ground, even getting your bear spray out of its holster and administering a blast take a lot of composure in the face of a charging bear when your instincts are screaming, "Run." You cannot outrun a grizzly, and your running can trigger the bear's "prey" instinct. For all these reasons it's important to do everything you can to avoid bear encounters and to practice the appropriate response so that it's instinctive should you get surprised.

Camping in Bear Country

Many areas where bears are known to roam have regulations that require campers to carry bear-proof canisters for their food. These canisters are made from hard plastic and have been proven to keep bears out. The downside of bear canisters is that they are heavy and take up a lot of room in your pack. If you are also carrying a full packraft setup, you'll need a high-volume backpack to carry all your gear.

Other options for food storage include the Ursack, a stuff sack made of bulletproof Spectra material that has been shown to keep bears out. Ursacks are very effective if they are shut properly. They are also light-weight and much easier to pack. For these reasons, many packrafters prefer to use Ursacks when traveling in bear country. Be sure to follow the directions on your Ursack. They need to be closed with a specific knot and tied to a tree or bush so that a bear cannot carry the bag off. *Note:* Ursacks are not approved for use in all parts of the United States, so check with land managers to make sure they are approved for the area where you plan to travel.

If you don't have a bear canister or an Ursack, you can hang your food to keep it out of reach of bears. Throw bags work well for constructing bear hangs. But beware: Bears are wily and often good climbers, especially in areas where they see a lot of people. To be secure, your food must be 10 feet off the ground and at least 4 feet away from the trunk of the tree or any overhanging branches.

In addition to storing your food properly, it's best to separate your kitchen and food storage area by 100 yards or so from your sleeping area to ensure that a curious bear doesn't stumble into you if food smells lure it into camp. Keep all your smelly stuff stored with your food in the kitchen area. That includes toothpaste, sunscreen, and bug repellent—anything that doesn't smell like nature.

Some people further separate themselves from cooking smells by stopping to eat along the trail or river and then traveling for another hour or so to ensure they aren't anywhere near their kitchen when they go to sleep.

Finally, if you are traveling in bear country, think about the food you bring with you. Oily, smelly foods—smoked fish, tuna, etc.—attract not only bears but also rodents and birds that might be looking for a quick and easy meal. Even after you've eaten those foods, you are left with smelly packaging that will add lingering odors to your pack for the rest of your trip. Double-bagging these items in plastic will help, but if you are really worried about food odor, avoid stinky food in your menu.

CHAPTER TEN

MAINTENANCE, REPAIR, AND MODIFICATIONS

THE BEAUTY OF PACKRAFTS IS THAT THEY ARE LIGHTWEIGHT. THEIR downside is that they are lightweight. Lightweight materials are less durable than the heavier stuff used to make big rafts or inflatable kayaks. You'll be amazed at how sturdy your packraft is, but it takes care to avoid the effects of wear and tear.

To help avoid rips and holes, pay attention to your gear. Watch where you put your raft down or what you are heading toward when you float downriver. Sticks and sharp rocks are not a packraft's friends, so avoid them if you can. Don't sit on the top of your raft when it is resting on rocks or vegetation, and don't let it sit out fully inflated in the hot sun. Clean your gear when you are done, and store it properly. Maintain zippers. Routinely look over your gear before you put it away to check for wear spots. The better you take care of your equipment, the better it will work for you.

Ultimately, no matter how careful you are, at some point in your packrafting career, it's likely that something will break or tear. For this reason, it's important to always carry a repair kit and know how to use it.

Before you begin mixing up your glue or cutting out a patch, think through what exactly needs to be done to make your repair. If you rush ahead, you may waste materials or find that your glue has become too tacky because you've taken longer than anticipated. Repair work needs to be done methodically to ensure it's done properly and that your packraft will hold air when the fix is completed.

Packrafts are designed to be lightweight and portable, which means the fabrics from which they are made tend to be a little less durable than those used for bigger, beefier whitewater rafts.

PACKRAFT REPAIR

Materials

Packraft manufacturers use different materials. It's important to know what material is used in your packraft model, as this will affect things like the type of glue you use and how you prepare the material for patching.

Finding the Leak

Before you start looking for a leak because your boat is soft, make sure you've tempered your raft, or reinflated it after submerging it in cold water. Warm air condenses when it cools, so that hot air you blew into the raft takes up less room when it's been on the water for a little while. You may have to add air several times before your packraft is firm enough.

Basic Field Repair Kit

- Alcohol wipes or a mini-dropper bottle of isopropyl alcohol to clean the site of your repair for better stick. The upside to wipes is that they are small and light; the downside is that they can dry out over time. If you go this route, replace the wipes in your repair kit every season.
- Tenacious Tape or Patch-N-Go tape to provide a temporary repair for holes in the tubes.
- Tyvek for temporary patches to textured fabrics, such as the back side of two-sided tubing or the floor of the packraft.
- Aquaseal for sealing small holes and seams and for reinforcing stitches. Aquaseal needs to cure for at least 12 hours.
- Scissors.
- Needle and unwaxed dental floss (A hospital suture kit works great if you can secure one.)
- Spare valve cap or inflation tip.
- Small-size permanent marker.
- Handful of zip ties.

Note: For sidecountry trips where you can walk out if your raft is damaged, go light and carry just alcohol wipes and tape in your repair kit.

A good basic repair kit includes the following: a multi-tool with scissors, a spare valve cap, urethane patches, alcohol, zipper lube, Aquaseal, Patch-N-Go patches, and a lighter with Tyvek tape wrapped around it.

Home Repair

- Carmo PVC–Pur Seal or Stabond for bonding fabrics together. These glues are used for securing patches for permanent repairs and for adding D-rings or tie-downs. Full cure takes 24 hours.
- Urethane patching material.

Next check the air valves. Sometimes you'll lose air through the valve if it is not closed tightly. All valves should be snug to ensure they are airtight.

Once you've determined that you do in fact have a leak, pull your raft out of the water and move to a quiet place where you can hear air escaping. Inspect your raft carefully. Sometimes your hole will be obvious. Be sure to look closely at seams and along the floor of the raft. Pay close

Packrafts are surprisingly durable and will hold up to lots of abuse. Most of the time damage is caused by sharps sticks or objects rather than rocks or hard use.

attention to high-stress areas, such as seat attachments, grab loops, and where your feet rest on the tubes, as these spots are subject to a lot of wear and tear.

If you suspect you've found the culprit, spit on the spot or use soapy water to help detect bubbles escaping through the hole. If this doesn't work, take your raft to calm water and submerge sections of it beneath the surface to look for a stream of bubbles rising from the hole.

If the leak is letting water into your cockpit—rather than allowing air to escape the tubes or seat—pour water into the raft and tilt it on its side to see if you can find the hole. Don't expect a big flow of water. You're looking for little bubbles slipping through. Flip to the other side and do the same thing.

Once you've found your hole, mark the spot. If you have a permanent marker, use that. If not, place a finger over the hole and head to a place where you can make your repairs.

Let the raft dry before you begin working on it.

Temporary Repairs

If you are on the water in the middle of a run, you won't have time to go through the lengthy process of making a permanent repair, which generally takes 12 to 24 hours for the glue to cure properly.

For quick fixes, repair tape works best. Packrafters have used just about any kind of tape for making a hasty fix, but the best brands seem to be Tenacious Tape—which carries both tape and ready-made patches—and Patch-N-Go tape for smooth surfaces, and Gorilla, Tyvek, or Tenacious tape on textured ones.

Start by drying the site thoroughly and cleaning it with an alcohol wipe if you have one. Otherwise, wipe it off with a lint-free cloth. Deflate the raft for all repair work. If you apply tape to an inflated raft, it will wrinkle when the raft is deflated, creating folds that allow air to escape.

For pinprick-size holes, cut a circular piece of tape with a 1-inch diameter. Make sure the tape stays clean, especially along its edge. Apply it to the raft and rub it into place, forcing out all air bubbles and warming the patch with friction to help the glue adhere more effectively.

For temporary treatment of larger tears, follow the same basic procedure outlined above, but you want to put tape on both sides of the tear if you can access the inside of the packraft's tube. The coating on some packrafts is the same inside and out; on others the inside does not have the shiny urethane coating. Patch-N-Go won't stick to the uncoated fabric, so you will need to use something like Gorilla Tape or even duct tape in a pinch for the uncoated side. Uncoated fabric absorbs water, so for the repair to be effective, you may need to let the raft dry for a while.

Cut your tape so that it extends roughly 1 inch beyond the edges of the tear. Round off the edges. Slide the tape through the hole carefully and rub the raft material down onto the tape to secure it in place. Then place a patch made from Tenacious, Tyvek, or Patch-N-Go tape on the outside of the tube and rub aggressively to warm it up and seal the hole.

For bigger tears, place strips of tape perpendicularly across the tear to hold it together like you would use Steri-Strips to close a wound, then cover with a patch.

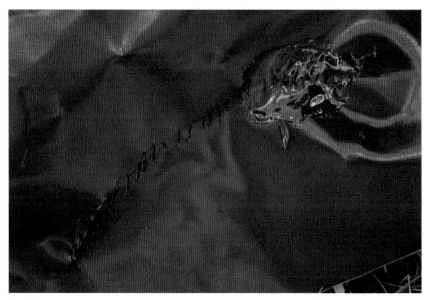

For bigger tears, sew the edges together with unwaxed dental floss or suture material and then cover with a thin layer of Seam Grip or Aquaseal.

Better yet, if you are carrying a needle and thread, you can sew the tear shut. Pull the edges of the tear together without overlapping. Stitch the two edges together, taking care to keep the fabric from puckering. Take your time, and make the stitches tight and close together. Once the tear is sewn shut, cover it with a layer of Aquaseal and let it sit overnight or for a minimum of 12 hours to cure. A sewn repair like this is a permanent repair.

Tyvek tape is for temporary repairs only. If you keep it on too long, it is hard to remove and leaves a sticky residue that makes applying a permanent patch difficult. So when you return from your packraft trip, remove the tape and put on a permanent patch. Tenacious Tape patches can stay in place indefinitely if put on properly, making this the field repair of choice since it is basically permanent.

Author's Tip

AIRE's BAKraft is made of an entirely different material than more traditional packrafts. AIRE recommends using Tear-Aid tape for sealing holes in the BAKraft. For more information on fixing a BAKraft, go to the AIRE website: aire.com.

Permanent Fixes

For more permanent repairs, you will need to allow time for the glue to cure. Typically this takes around 12 hours for Aquaseal and 24 for other glues, such as Stabond.

The basic procedure is similar to that for temporary fixes, except instead of tape you will be applying urethane patches. Most packrafts come with a small piece of the raft's material that you can cut into a custom-sized patch. Or you can buy repair patches from NRS.

Clean and prep the site with an alcohol pad and then let the raft dry thoroughly.

For a pinprick hole, all you need to do is dab a small blob (about ⅛ inch thick) of Aquaseal over the hole. Lay the raft flat so the glue won't run, and let it dry for 12 hours.

If you have a tear or a bigger hole, you'll want to use a patch.

Use a piece of 180-grit sandpaper to roughen up a small area around the hole. You just want to dull the shine of the material, not grind it down to expose the interior threads. Wipe the spot clean with an alcohol wipe and let dry. Mix the adhesive with accelerator to speed up the curing process. Different boat manufacturers recommend different glues. Stabond and Carmo PVC–Pur Seal are two reputable brands. Coat the surface of the raft and the underside of the patch with a thin layer of glue. Let the glue dry for 30 minutes and then apply a second layer. Let it dry again—this time for 15 minutes or until it is tacky to the touch.

Dry Suit Repair

The principles for raft repair and dry suit repair are similar. The biggest question will be determining the best glue for a patch if you have a tear. Aquaseal will seal pinprick holes without a patch. Tears to your dry suit's gaskets need to be fixed right away to prevent them from ripping further as you pull the dry suit on and off.

To fix a tear in the gasket, clean the site with an alcohol wipe and let the moisture evaporate off. Cut a piece of Tear-Aid tape twice the length of the rip plus roughly 1 inch extra. You want the tape to extend beyond the bottom of the tear by ½ inch and to fold over the top of the gasket so that it holds the rip on both sides. Trim the edges so the tape is oval shaped.

Place the gasket on a flat surface with the tear exposed. Peel back half the Tear-Aid tape backing and place it ½ inch below the bottom of the tear; press down on the tape, smoothing it out as you work it toward the edge of the gasket. Once the first half of the tape is secure, remove the rest of the backing. Fold the tape over the edge of the gasket and smooth it down on the back side so that the tear is sealed by tape on both sides.

Tear-Aid provides a temporary fix. Keep an eye on it as you pull the gasket on and off. The gasket will stretch more than the tape, so it can come unstuck if you are not careful. If this happens, rub the tape back into place. If the tape has lost its stick, replace the patch.

When you get home, replace the gasket. Tear-Aid won't last long term.

Press the patch to the tube carefully, making sure not to get any wrinkles in the fabric. Rub aggressively to warm up the glue so the patch sticks better. Let the raft sit for 24 hours for the glue to cure. You can get back on the water earlier if needed; just know the patch will not be as strong as it will be once the glue has cured and therefore will be easier to scrape off if you bump up against a rock.

Make sure you apply the glue thinly. Too thick and it makes the patch bulky and easier to pull off.

VALVES

If air is escaping through a valve on your boat, check first to see that it is clean of dirt and sand. You may also want to double-check to make sure the valve is screwed shut tightly.

If you are still losing air, check to see if there is a leak around the base or the welding. If you find bubbles coming up here, you can seal the hole with Aquaseal. Clean the area first and let it dry. When you put the Aquaseal on the hole, try to work it down into the fabric as best you can. Let the Aquaseal dry.

If the valve itself is leaking, your repair will depend on the type of valve. For Alpacka's top-off valves, you may need to replace the mouthpiece if you have a spare tip in your repair kit. If you do not have one, you can fold the valve stem in half and wrap it tightly in place with string to keep air from escaping for a temporary fix.

For the main valve cap, check to see if the O-ring is intact. If it isn't, you can jury-rig an O-ring with a bicycle tube. If you don't have that, take a plastic bag and screw it in with the valve cap to help maintain a seal. In an emergency, you can Aquaseal the valve cap in place and use the top-off valve for inflation and deflation.

If you have lost your valve cap, you can use your inflation bag nozzle to secure a plastic bag over the valve opening and create a seal.

ZIPPERS

More and more packrafts are coming with waterproof zippers. Your dry suit will also have one. These zippers need to be handled carefully to keep them functioning smoothly. Waterproof zippers are one of the most expensive and time-consuming parts of your raft or dry suit to replace.

Keep the zipper clean. NRS recommends using McNett Zip Care for cleaning. Zip Care comes with an applicator brush on top of the container, so you just apply it to the zipper and wipe away any excess fluid after you are done. You can also use a toothbrush and warm, soapy water to clean the zipper. The benefit of McNett's Zip Care is that it cleans and lubes at the same time, enhancing the movement of the zipper.

Brush and clean your zipper after every use if you are paddling in silty or sandy water.

You should also wax the zipper regularly. NRS recommends McNett Zip Tech for keeping dry suit or raft zippers supple and sliding well. Apply the wax or lube evenly along the zipper, and open and close it a couple of times to work the wax in between the teeth.

The number-one cause of zipper failure occurs when the zipper gets bent, causing breaks in the material between the teeth. To prevent this, store waterproof zippers so they lie flat. If you are transporting your raft or dry suit, try not to bend the zipper too tightly. Pack it loosely and, if possible, without folds or kinks to help maximize its lifespan.

PADDLE REPAIR

If you break or, worse, lose your paddle, you have few options. Many packrafters carry a spare paddle in the group just in case. Permitted rivers often require groups to carry spare paddles, and on big rivers it's essential that you have a real paddle to navigate whitewater, so it's wise to carry a spare even if it's not required.

One trick for creating a lightweight spare paddle is to cut blades from high molecular weight (HMW) polyethylene with holes drilled in one end. HMW plastic is available in sheets and can be cut to size; look for sources online. Use your paddle blade as a template. The blades can then be attached to a trekking pole or stick with zip ties and used in an emergency.

In a pinch there are a few other things you can try to get you through the trip.

One is to splint a broken shaft with either a tent pole or a piece of wood. Tightly lash the splint in place on either end. If the shaft is too rough to grip, paddle in neoprene gloves. Make sure you try gripping the paddle before you lash it together. If the shaft is too fat, you won't be able to hold onto your paddle properly.

On small rivers you can use your hands to paddle. Packrafts maneuver easily without requiring a lot of power. Hand paddling will not work in big whitewater or for long stretches of flatwater. In these situations, you may need to get out and walk.

The ferrules on your paddle can become too tight or too loose with wear. To help prevent this, dip your paddle shaft in clean water and wipe off dirt before putting it together. This will help keep dirt and sand out of the ferrule, where it can wear down the shaft.

If the ferrule in your breakdown paddle is too tight, wipe it clean and see if that helps. If you still have trouble putting the paddle together, you can gently sand the male end with 600-grit sandpaper. Make sure to clean the shaft carefully before you try to put the pieces together.

If the ferrule is too loose, you can dip the male end into lacquer or varnish. Polyurethane works well. After the varnish or lacquer is dry, sand it down with 400-grit sandpaper to remove any tackiness or if the fit is too tight. You can keep sanding until you get the desired fit.

ADDING D-RINGS AND TIE-DOWNS TO YOUR RAFT

Adding tie-down patches or D-rings can be useful modifications to your packraft. You can use them to make more attachment points and for securing thigh straps. It's important to use the proper glue to ensure that the patches will hold. Glue type will be determined by the materials to be attached. Most packrafts—except for AIRE's BAKraft—are made from urethane-coated nylon. For urethane, the best glue is Stabond.

Materials needed for gluing on tie-downs:

- Stabond and accelerator
- PVC cleaner: methyl ethyl ketone (MEK) or toluol (toluene)
- Roller

- Patches or D-rings
- 180-grit sandpaper
- Permanent marker
- Disposable container with a lid (margarine tub works well)
- Small, disposable brush

Preparation

Make sure you set up your project in a well-ventilated area and wear chemical-resistant gloves to do this work. Work on a deflated packraft.

Determine where you want to apply the patches on your packraft. Once you have figured that out, hold the patch in place and trace it with a permanent marker. Remove the patch. Use sandpaper to rough up the site. Your goal is to remove the fabric's shine. Don't sandpaper down to the threads.

Once you've roughened up the tube, clean the surface of both the packraft and the patch with PVC cleaner and let dry thoroughly.

Mix the glue with the accelerator in an empty margarine container using a 10-to-1 ratio. Keep the lid on when you are not using the glue to prevent it from drying out.

Using a small brush, apply an even, thin layer of glue to the patch site on the raft tube and to the underside of the patch. Let the glue dry for 10 to 30 minutes, depending on conditions. The glue is dry enough when you can feel the adhesion but your gloved finger does not stick.

Apply a second thin, even coat and let sit for 5 to 10 minutes, until the adhesive is tacky but not visibly wet. Immediately press the patch onto the tube, starting at one edge and slowly pressing the patch down. Using a roller or the handle of a screwdriver, roll the patch from the center out to the sides to force air bubbles out. Wipe up excess glue with a lint-free towel.

You can use a heat gun or hair dryer to add a little heat to the glue. You don't need much. If the heat feels too hot on your skin, it is too hot for your packraft. The glue is activated at body temperature, so hold the heat source about 8 to 10 inches away while you heat the site. Let the raft sit for 24 to 48 hours to allow a complete cure.

ADDING THIGH STRAPS

Many packrafters are installing thigh straps into their packrafts. According to Luc Mehl in his blog post "Pimp My Packraft," thigh straps are the equivalent of clipless pedals on your bike—you get a better connection with your boat, which translates into more responsiveness and power. Thigh straps give you more control and allow you to tilt the boat or lift a tube by applying pressure through your legs. Thigh straps also help your packraft track better and allow you to use a hip snap to stay upright when a wave or hole sucks your tube down.

There are a number of different systems for installing thigh straps in your boat. The tried-and-true method has an attachment point near the hip on the packraft tube and by your foot on the floor, but people are experimenting with new ways to rig their thigh straps to enhance their boat's responsiveness and make the straps safer. It's worth doing some research online if you are an aggressive boater who intends to roll your packraft in whitewater. For those who are happy in more moderate water and are looking for thigh straps to improve control rather than to roll their boat, the two-point system described below works great.

Using thigh straps is like using clipless pedals on a bicycle or tightening your shoes for a run. They give you more control and a better feel for your packraft.

Materials

- **Four tie-down patches (two for each strap).** You can find a variety of tie-downs on the market. Alpacka makes a lightweight, inexpensive option, but they are not as sturdy as larger PVC or urethane-coated D-ring patches made by companies like NRS or AIRE. If you are an aggressive boater and plan to be paddling challenging whitewater, go for the D-ring patches. For easier whitewater, the lighter-weight option sold by Alpacka will suffice.

- **Glue.** Stabond U-148 glue is strong and durable and is recommended by most packrafters. You can also use Loctite Vinyl, Fabric & Plastic Flexible Adhesive, although its reputation for security is not as good as Stabond's.

- **Straps.** A number of whitewater boat manufacturers like AIRE and NRS make padded thigh straps that are comfortable and secure and include a quick-release buckle for emergencies. Recent AIRE models feature metal cams for adjusting the length of the strap, which adds to their weight. If your straps have metal cams, you may want to replace them with plastic buckles to lighten your load. For easier boating, 1-inch webbing straps with plastic adjustable buckles work well. They will be lighter, but not as comfortable as padded thigh straps.

  On average, thigh straps and the D-rings needed to hold them in place will add about 1 pound, 5 ounces to your overall packraft weight.

Installment Instructions

Inflate your boat and seat, and sit down inside. Take one thigh strap and place the padded end near your hip, the other end down by your feet on the floor. The foot tie-down patch should be placed on the floor of your packraft, up under the front tube as far forward as possible and to the outside of where your foot will rest when you are boating. Once you've figured out where you want your foot tie-down to go, it helps to have someone hold that end in place while you determine where to place the one for your hip.

Place the rear attachment point for your thigh straps slightly above your hip. This packraft has the thigh strap and backrest tied off at the same point.

With the foot end secure, pull the strap back and hold it on the tube by your hip. On an Alpacka raft, you'll want the tie-down patch to go above the intake valve. On other packraft models, place the tie-down slightly above and behind the crest of your hip. Pull the strap so it is snug and holds your leg close to the tube.

When you have found the appropriate spot for each tie-down patch, mark it by tracing the outline of the patch with a permanent marker onto the tube and floor. Do this for both sides.

Deflate your boat and follow the instructions for gluing in tie-downs described above. Allow the glue to cure before attaching your thigh straps and testing their efficacy on a river.

CHAPTER ELEVEN

TRIP PLANNING

So you have the gear, you've practiced the skills, you know how to fix things if they break, and you are ready to go. Wilderness packrafting adventures are what make packrafting unique. There's nothing quite like hiking and boating your way through mountains or deserts. It's fun and exciting and gets you into beautiful places.

Your packraft opens up new worlds to explore, such as Bosnia's Neretva River.

The best trips combine hiking and paddling about equally, although obviously that depends on personal preference. Some areas like the Bob Marshall Wilderness in Montana and the Brooks Range in Alaska lend themselves to hiking from one drainage to another. Other trips tend to be more about walking to the headwaters of a river and floating out. The beauty of packrafting is that you can do what you want. If you get sick of boating, pack up your raft and hike. If the river is too small or too difficult, you can walk. If your feet are tired and you'd rather get your pack off your back, float on downstream.

PICKING A DESTINATION

Finding Route Information

The best place to start your dreaming is to go online and search "packrafting." Your search will bring up all sorts of information, including detailed trip reports from packrafters around the world. These reports give you

With a packraft you can hike over mountain passes like this one in Alaska's Brooks Range to access a new river.

You can find information about packrafting adventures around Jackson Hole, Wyoming, on Forrest McCarthy's blog.

plenty of options and guidelines for planning your first—or hundredth—packrafting adventure.

Roman Dial's book *Packrafting!* contains a number of stories about his packrafting adventures, or you can check his website, The Roaming Dials (packrafting.blogspot.com), for lots of ideas on where to go and how to figure out logistics for a specific destination. Roman has packrafted all over the world and pioneered many packraft descents, so he's a great resource for those of you just getting into the sport.

Likewise, Forrest McCarthy (forrestmccarthy.blogspot.com) writes about his adventures with his packraft on his blog; he also has an online guidebook for packraft excursions around Jackson Hole, Wyoming. Luc Mehl's website has trip information as well as tips for "pimping out" your packraft, and the Facebook group Packrafters' Liberation Front often has posts detailing adventures its members have taken. Australian Mark Oates has a Facebook page—Wildabout Packrafting—where you can find videos and trip reports from all over but particularly from Tasmania, which is reputed to be a haven for packrafting. Oates also rents packrafts for people looking for an adventure Down Under.

The American Packrafting Association (packrafting.org) is a great place to go for the most up-to-date news on packrafting issues, such as access, permits, and other management concerns that might affect your trip. APA also maintains a forum that allows members to ask questions, seek advice, and find paddling partners. The group hosts a roaming packrafters' rendezvous every summer as well. The rendezvous attracts more packrafters every year and is a great place to meet other boaters, get advice on the latest techniques and equipment, and take a rescue clinic or go for a packrafting excursion with a gang of new friends.

These are just a few of the resources available online if you are looking for information. As the sport grows, its number of participants increases, and more and more of them are posting information about their adventures online. Just play around with your search engine and you are likely to come up with other sites offering ideas for your next trip. Of course, as with all Internet information, use your judgment. You may not want to replicate all the packraft trips people have taken.

Some rivers, like the North Fork of the Virgin in Utah, are only boatable in years when water levels are high, so you have to do your homework if you want to packraft them.

The Bob Marshall Wilderness Area in Montana is ideal packrafting country with lots of rivers to paddle and wild country to hike.

Packraft Destinations in the United States

- The Bob Marshall Wilderness in Montana is an ideal spot to create a packrafting loop that includes rafting on Class II or III—even Class IV in places—whitewater and spectacular hiking.
- The Brooks Range in Alaska has tons of potential for wild travel through the Arctic on rivers and off-trail across the tundra.
- Canyonlands National Park, Escalante National Monument, and the Dirty Devil in Utah and the North Rim of the Grand Canyon in Arizona allow packrafters the chance to combine canyoneering, canyon hiking, and packrafting through spectacular red-rock deserts.
- The Absaroka Mountains in Wyoming have options for loops or through-hikes that range from a few days to a couple of weeks surrounded by sheer cliffs, lush meadows, abundant wildlife, and very few people.

These are just a few of the areas that are seeing lots of packrafting exploration in the American West. You can find more online. And packrafting is not limited to North America. Boaters are using their packrafts to explore all over the world. So use your imagination, do some research, and find your own exciting adventure.

The Alatna River is a Wild and Scenic River in Gates of the Arctic National Park in Alaska. The river has been called one of the most beautiful in the United States and is ideal for packrafting.

A number of outfitters around the country are offering guided pack-rafting trips. If you are new to the sport and don't have a lot of time to put into planning, going with a guide on your first adventure could be a good way to go.

SEASON

Rivers are seasonal, and many are only boatable in spring when the water is high. Exactly when spring is depends on where you are boating. In the United States, spring starts in March and April in the mid-Atlantic states; in Alaska it occurs in June.

For the United States, the US Geological Survey (USGS) provides online water levels from gauges on rivers throughout the country. These gauges may not be specific to the section of river you hope to boat, but they can give you an indication of water levels in the area.

Local outfitters are also a good source of information on water levels and boating conditions.

Spring runoff and flood-level flows can make boating dangerous, while it can be impossible when the water is too low. Check on water levels before you commit to a packrafting trip.

MAPS

Some rivers have guidebooks that indicate rapids, falls, and other obstacles, but for most wilderness river trips you will be limited to a topographic map.

The challenge is determining whether a blue line indicating a watercourse on the map translates into a river you can boat. You can get a sense of the size of the river by looking at its catchment area. But your best bet for deciding if packrafting will be feasible is to pull up the area on Google Earth. Google Earth allows you to see what the river looks like. If it's a boulder-choked maelstrom, it's probably not a good option for a packrafting trip.

USGS topographic maps are a good place to start when planning your packrafting expedition. They provide detailed information about the landscape, though they may not tell you much about the nature of the river itself.

Maps also allow you to determine a river's gradient, which can indicate how turbulent or difficult the run might be. For example, if you have a contour line on a map with 100-foot contour intervals that crosses the river at Mile 1 and again at Mile 10, the mileage difference is 10. Ten divided into 100 equals a drop of 10 feet per mile.

A gradient of 1 to 5 feet per mile is generally easy cruising. Five to 10 gets a bit more exciting—say Class II or maybe III whitewater. Above 10 feet per mile, you should expect more challenging whitewater. At gradients greater than 20 feet per mile, you will probably encounter Class IV and up.

But gradient can be deceiving. Sometimes the drop you calculate on a map comes in one waterfall. Other times it is spread out over the entire distance. To help get a sense of the river's character, look more closely at the contour lines. Canyons, indicated by contour lines stacked up tightly on either side of the river corridor, tend to constrict rivers and often create rapids as the current is forced into a narrow channel. Canyons can also mean portaging may be difficult.

You may not always be able to detect a waterfall on a topographic map. Do your homework, and ask people familiar with the area what to expect before you launch and head downstream.

A couple of contour lines close together as they cross the river may indicate a waterfall. But remember, a 4-foot drop can feel like a waterfall in a packraft, and those kinds of drops are not going to show up on a map.

ROCK TYPE

It can be strange to consider rock type when talking about boating, but the geology of an area has a huge impact on how navigable its rivers will be. In general, craggy granitic mountain ranges tend to have steep, bouldery rivers that can be hard to boat, while sedimentary rocks often weather more gradually and create rivers with less gradient and fewer boulders. An example of this can be found in Wyoming. The granitic Wind River Range has a few rivers that can be run, but most are very difficult and often require long portages to get around unrunnable sections. The nearby Absaroka Mountains are made from volcanic sediments that erode into high flat-topped plateaus and deep U-shaped valleys with perfect packraftable rivers. Not that these rivers don't have rapids; they do. But they don't have the same steep gradient that you find in the Winds.

PERMITS

Many rivers have a permit system that controls the number of boaters allowed on the river at any given time. These rivers include sections of the Salmon River in Idaho, the Colorado River through the Grand Canyon, Colorado's Yampa River, and sections of the Green River in Utah and Colorado, to name a few. Permitted rivers can be part of a packrafting adventure, but you need to abide by the regulations and have a permit to boat them legally.

Permits are usually given out through a lottery that occurs months before the river season. American Whitewater maintains a comprehensive list of permitted rivers in North America. You can go to american whitewater.org/content/River/list-permits/ to look up different rivers and get information on how to go about obtaining a permit. Some rivers require lottery permits only in the high season. At other times of the year, you can run the river with a permit secured by calling the land management agency in charge and making a reservation over the phone, which can be a great way to get on a river like the Salmon in the off-season.

Permit Requirements

River requirements were created for big rafting expeditions, which means some of the items you are expected to carry do not work for packrafters who plan to hike. The American Packraft Association (APA) has been working with land managers in charge of these permits to find ways to modify the regulations so that packrafters can meet the requirements and still be able to pack up and backpack with all their gear.

In general, river managers have proven to be amenable to working with packrafters on the regulations. If you want to run a permitted river, check with APA to see if it has any information on that particular river and whether the managers are open to packrafting. Or call up the land manager for the river in question to discuss your trip plans. Be polite and flexible if you want them to be polite and flexible.

Here are some ideas for dealing with permit requirements:

- Fire pans are required on most permitted rivers even if you have no plan to build a fire. On some but not all rivers, packrafters can use a lightweight aluminum roasting pan to serve as a fire pan. Currently this practice is not acceptable in Grand Canyon National Park. APA is working with park management to figure out a lightweight fire pan option, so this problem may be remedied in the near future.
- Portable potties—"groovers" in river lingo—are another item required on most rivers that are totally unworkable for a packrafter, as the typical groover would never fit in a backpack. Ask land managers if you can carry WAG Bags, RESTOP toilet kits, or another portable bag system for disposing of human waste coupled with some kind of container (such as a plastic peanut butter jar) or dry bag to carry your waste out.
- Most regulated rivers require a spare paddle for every craft, but some managers are willing to allow packrafters to carry a spare for every couple of boats. You can also consider bringing paddle blades that can be fitted onto the end of a trekking pole for a spare.
- Many river regulations require a spare life jacket for every boat. Extra lifejackets are bulky and consume space. Check with the river managers to see if you can compromise and bring a spare for the entire group.

Many popular rivers, such as sections of the Green River, require packrafters to have permits during peak season.

HOW FAR CAN YOU GO?

When mapping out a packrafting route, you need to consider your hiking as well as your boating mileage. On a flat, buff trail, backpackers average about 3 miles per hour. Off-trail or on rugged trails, your speed drops to closer to 2 miles per hour. Add elevation gain—1,000 feet of elevation gain equates to about an additional mile of travel time—and you can come up with a rough estimate of how long it will take you to travel from point A to point B on foot. For example, if your route covers 6 miles and gains 2,000 feet, you can expect to be hiking for about 4 hours, or the equivalent of 8 miles.

As you gain experience, you can modify these calculations based on your own travel times, but these guidelines give you a good place to start.

Your river travel speed can be trickier to calculate in advance. The speed of the current controls your speed of travel. As a general rule, you can expect to average around 2 to 4 miles per hour on a Class II or III river. High water may speed that up considerably unless you have lots of

On trails you can cover as much as 3 miles per hour. Once you get off-trail, your speed will drop. Be prepared to travel 2 miles or less per hour if you are encountering lots of obstacles and stream crossings.

Your river speed is determined by the speed of the current as well as the number of obstacles you encounter. Most packrafters average between 12 and 18 miles per day.

Big-volume rivers with lots of current can make it easier to log lots of miles during the day. This packrafter is floating by historic Mostar in Bosnia. Packrafting adventures are not limited to wilderness trips.

obstacles to avoid or portage. Flatwater rivers will slow you way down. Headwinds will also affect your speed. And rapids that require scouting or take time to run can add hours to your day.

In general, packrafters can comfortably travel 12 to 18 miles per day on a river. That's not to say you cannot do more, but you may find you are paddling dawn to dusk if you tackle a bigger chunk of river time.

The good thing about packrafting is that in many ways your paddling day will be a rest day for your legs and feet, so you'll feel revived when you get off the river and start hiking again.

GEAR

Wilderness packrafting trips require a lot of equipment, which can mean your pack weight will be heavy if you don't plan for the trip carefully. Going light allows you to be more comfortable on the trail, makes it easier to pound out the miles, and minimizes wear and tear on your body.

To help with organization, lay out all the gear you think you want to bring on the floor. Being able to inspect items can help you pare down

Your gear will vary according to the weather and water temperatures you expect to encounter on your trip. This photograph shows technical gear for a cold-weather trip. It does not include clothing or food.

what you need. If you are new to the backpacking game, talk to friends who have more experience and ask them to help you come up with a gear list. Do some research online or at the library. We've included sample gear lists in this book to help get you started.

Keep a list on your computer of the equipment you opt to take on a trip. Include the number of days, miles, and other logistical information on that list. When you get back from your trip, make notes. Delete items you did not use or mark the reasons you did not use a particular item. Make a note of what you missed and what items were essential to your comfort and safety. These notes will help make your next trip easier.

Packrafting Gear

You don't have a lot of wiggle room in your packrafting gear. The primary factor in determining your essentials will be whether you intend to paddle flatwater or whitewater.

The more efficient and careful your packing, the less weight and volume you'll have to carry in your pack or on your boat.

Going Light Principles

- **Avoid redundancy in your gear.** If you can use one item for several things, great. You don't need a river knife and a kitchen knife, for example. You can eat and drink out of your pot. The more multipurpose gear you carry, the less gear you carry.
- **Share.** Talk to your team and figure out what gear you can share to avoid duplications. You only need one repair kit, for instance, and usually doubling up in a lightweight shelter is more efficient than carrying two one-person tents. Cooking together helps minimize your load too.
- **Invest in lightweight gear.** Today's equipment is a lot lighter than it used to be. If you are carrying a pack or tent you bought twenty years ago, it's time to update your equipment. Take advantage of high-tech materials and designs to shave pounds off your pack weight.
- **Need less.** Don't pack items "just in case." If you've never worn that third upper-body layer you always bring just in case, leave it behind. You don't need it. If it gets cold, go to bed. Be honest with yourself and brutal in your packing. Leave behind the extras. Bring only items that are essential to your health and safety. Your feet will thank you for it.

If you plan to paddle flat or mellow water in warm weather, you can go light and leave your helmet and dry suit at home.

Flatwater boaters can go light. Flatwater packrafts weigh a fraction of whitewater models. Furthermore, you can wear an inflatable life vest and leave your helmet behind if you are not going to be running rapids.

But if you plan to run Class III rapids or above, you need to include:

- Packraft and inflation system
- Type III PFD
- Whitewater boating helmet
- Breakdown paddle
- Appropriate clothing (more on that later)
- Throw bag
- Packraft repair kit
- 2–3 carabiners

This setup will weigh roughly 15 pounds. It's not the place to cut weight. You need to do that with your backpacking gear and your food.

Backpacking Gear

For organizational purposes, it makes sense to divide your gear into group gear that you share among your team and personal gear that is only for you. Some people like to be totally self-sufficient when they go backpacking, meaning they'll bring everything from a shelter to their stove to their personal clothing. There are some advantages to this approach. You only have to worry about your own stuff then, and no one needs to be concerned about breaking or losing someone else's equipment. But when you go this route, you inevitably end up bringing more than you need, and as a result everyone's pack is heavier than necessary. Plus sharing meals with your teammates at the end of a long day adds to the camaraderie of the expedition.

Group gear includes all the stuff that can be shared: shelters, cooking gear, toilet kits, stoves, repair kits, first-aid kits, maps, etc. Lay this stuff out and divide it into piles, one for each team member. It's nice to take the individual's size into account when you are dividing up the gear. Big

You can shave weight off your pack by sharing gear and using equipment for more than one purpose. Here a breakdown paddle has been lashed together with ski straps to serve as the tent pole.

people should be able to carry more than little people, so try to consider that as you hand out loads.

Your trip will dictate just what group gear you need. You can use the list below to get started. Modify it according to your personal needs and objectives.

Group Camping Gear

Gear	
Sleeping	• Fly or lightweight tent. Bring the smallest, lightest size to accommodate your group. (You can forgo a full tent if you don't anticipate lots of bugs.)
Kitchen	• Stove with windscreen and fuel, lighter
	• 1 pot (size depends on group size)
	• Lightweight pot grips or wool gloves for handling hot items
	• Water bladder for carrying water
	• Hand washing/sanitizer soap
Latrine Kit	• Spade for digging catholes
	• Toilet paper, garbage bag for packing out used paper
	• Individual, commercially available sanitary bags for carrying out human waste (e.g., a WAG Bag) if required by permit
Camping in Bear Country	• Bear-proof canisters or Ursacks for food storage
	• Bear spray
	• Carrying firearms in the Arctic may be recommended in some places where polar bears are found. Check with local authorities.
Communications (These items are optional and depend on the remoteness of your trip.)	• Cell phone or satellite phone
	• Global positioning system (GPS) device
	• Spare batteries or portable electronic power source
	• Personal locator beacon (PLB)

Gear

Maps, Documents, etc.	• At least one set of maps stored in a waterproof bag
	• Copy of any necessary permits
	• Guidebook or route information, if available
First-Aid Kit	• See appendix A.
Drug Kit	• See appendix C.
Group Repair Kit	• See appendix D.

Backpacking Clothing

Making smart choices in your attire can mean the difference between joy and misery on a packrafting trip.

The principle of multiple-use gear extends to your clothing. Think about the way you use your layers, and try to come up with options that can be multipurpose. For example, a nylon buff can be used as a neck gaiter, a headband, or a lightweight hat. A mosquito shirt can serve as a windshirt. And you can always drape your sleeping bag around your shoulders for an extra insulating layer around camp.

This paddler is dressed for cold-water paddling on moderate water. She is not wearing a helmet and is using an inflatable PFD, both of which would be inappropriate on a harder river but help her save weight on a mellower one.

In warmer climates you can opt to wear rain gear or paddling jackets to keep off any splashing water without the unnecessary weight and waterproofness of a dry suit.

In general, the only difference when packing for a packrafting trip versus a regular backpacking trip is the fact that you need to factor in boating. In cold climates or cold water, you need clothing that will keep you warm (wet suit) or warm and dry (dry suit). These items add a couple of pounds to your pack weight but are essential to preventing hypothermia if you plan to paddle glacial rivers, in the early spring, or whenever you anticipate chilly, rainy weather.

For summer boating on easier mountain rivers, you can opt to paddle in your rain gear. To keep dry, make sure you zip the jacket all the way up to keep water from dribbling in. Push your insulating layer up to your elbow, and close the wrist fasteners on your rain jacket tightly to keep water from wicking up your arms. Even with these precautions, you are likely to get wet. If you plan to go this route (which will be lighter), consider bringing two sets of base layers—a wet and a dry set—so when you pull into camp after a long, cold day on the water, you can change into dry clothes. Obviously, you want to pay attention to pack weight, but a couple of ounces for dry layers will be worth it in certain conditions.

Taking Care of Your Feet

Figuring out what to wear on your feet on a packrafting trip can be tricky. Do you want camp shoes and hiking shoes? Neoprene, Gore-Tex, or super fluffy wool socks? Your goal should be to carry as little as possible to keep your feet warm and dry. Many packrafters opt not to bring camp shoes because of the added weight. Instead they carry Gore-Tex socks that fit over dry wool socks to wear inside their wet shoes while in camp. On the river it's nice to wear thick warm socks inside your dry suit. If you don't have a dry suit, Gore-Tex or neoprene socks can help keep your feet warm. In cold climates keep a pair of warm dry socks stashed in a plastic bag in your pack for use in camp or at night.

It can be hot paddling in the desert, but often the water is cold (especially dam-fed rivers like the Colorado through the Grand Canyon), and if you are deep in a canyon, the lack of sun can cool things down. Check with others who are familiar with the area about how you'll want to dress for paddling. You may want a wet or dry suit despite high air temperatures because of the cold water; on the other hand, you may find a bathing suit and rain gear sufficient.

And remember that your life jacket or a paddling jacket can be used as an extra layer around camp if the temperatures are unexpectedly cold.

Gear List

Your gear list will vary with every trip. It depends on your route, your goals, your destination, and your personal comfort level. The list below is an expanded list, intended to give you guidelines, not dictate what you need. The goal of most packrafters is to pare down their personal gear to an absolute minimum so their packs stay as light as possible.

As you gain experience, keep track of the equipment and clothing you did and did not use. On your next trip, you can leave the unnecessary things behind and shave more ounces off your load.

Personal Gear Checklist

Gear	Warm-Weather Camping	Cold-Weather Camping
Upper Body	1 synthetic base layer (mid- or lightweight)	2 synthetic or wool base layers (mid- or lightweight)
	1 lightweight pile, wool jacket or down sweater	1 insulating layer (down or synthetic filled, or heavyweight pile jacket) with hood
		1 down or pile vest or expedition-weight layer (optional)
	1 lightweight windshirt	1 lightweight windshirt
	1 rain jacket	1 rain jacket
	1 T-shirt (synthetic best)	
	1 synthetic sport bra or top (women); can serve as a T-shirt	1 synthetic sport bra or top (women)
Lower Body	1 pair synthetic or wool long underwear bottoms or lightweight polyester hiking pants	1 pair synthetic or wool long underwear bottoms (mid- or lightweight)
	1 pair rain pants	1 pair rain pants
	1 pair nylon shorts (can be zip-off hiking pants)	1 pair insulated pants or shelled polypropylene
Head	1 visor or sunhat	1 visor or sunhat (optional)
Layers	1 lightweight wool or pile hat (nice if it fits under your helmet)	1 wool or pile hat
		1 neck gaiter, scarf, or balaclava
		1 fuzzy rubber helmet liner (optional)
	1 bandana (optional)	1 bandana (optional)

Gear	Warm-Weather Camping	Cold-Weather Camping
Underwear	2–3 pairs (Technical fabrics work best for quick drying. Shorts with liners work well for some people.)	2–3 pairs (Technical fabrics work best for quick drying.)
Hand Layers	1 lightweight pair of gloves (wool or synthetic)	1–2 lightweight pairs of gloves (wool or synthetic) 1 pair of insulated gloves or mittens
Foot Layers	2–3 pairs wool or synthetic socks Hiking/boating shoes 1 pair gaiters (optional) (Lightweight nylon running gaiters work great.) 1 pair lightweight camp shoes, such as Crocs or sandals (optional) 1 pair neoprene socks or river booties (optional) Gore-Tex socks (optional)	3–4 pairs wool or synthetic socks Hiking/boating boots 1 pair gaiters (optional) 1 pair insulated booties or camp shoes (optional) 1 pair neoprene socks or river booties (optional) Gore-Tex socks (optional)
Boating Gear	Packraft, paddle, PFD, helmet Throw rope, whistle, knife Dry suit, wet suit, or paddling attire	Packraft, paddle, PFD, helmet Throw rope, whistle, knife Dry suit Neoprene gloves, mittens, or pogies
Sleeping Gear	1 sleeping pad (If you have an inflatable sleeping pad, be sure someone in your group has a repair kit.)	1 sleeping pad (If you have an inflatable sleeping pad, be sure someone in your group has a repair kit.)

Gear	Warm-Weather Camping	Cold-Weather Camping
	1 sleeping bag/quilt (weight temperature dependent)	1 sleeping bag/quilt (weight temperature dependent)
	Stuff sacks for pad and sleeping bag (optional)	Stuff sacks for pad and sleeping bag (optional)
Toiletries	Toothbrush, toothpaste comb, unwaxed dental floss with needle for emergency sewing repairs, personal hygiene products, contact lens solution, sunscreen, lip balm, etc.	Toothbrush, toothpaste comb, unwaxed dental floss with needle for emergency sewing repairs, personal hygiene products, contact lens solution, sunscreen, lip balm, etc.
Eating	1 lightweight 12- to 16-ounce cup for eating and drinking (titanium or silicon)	1 lightweight 12- to 16-ounce cup for eating and drinking (titanium or silicon)
	1 lightweight spoon	1 lightweight spoon
	1–2 1-liter water bottles or hydration system	1–2 1-liter water bottles or hydration system
Extras	Sunglasses with retaining strap for river use	Sunglasses with retaining strap for river use
	Water purification system (SteriPEN, Potable Aqua, or Aquamira)	Water purification system (SteriPEN, Potable Aqua, or Aquamira)
	Money, credit card, drivers license	Money, credit card, drivers license
	Book, notebook, pencil or pen (optional)	Book, notebook, pencil or pen (optional)
	Headlamp	Headlamp
	Lighter or matches packed in a waterproof bag or container	Lighter or matches packed in a waterproof bag or container
	Camera (optional)	Camera (optional)
	Trekking poles (optional)	Trekking poles (optional)

Gear	Warm-Weather Camping	Cold-Weather Camping
	Binoculars (optional)	Binoculars (optional)
	Spare batteries for all electronic devices, or a portable solar-panel recharger	Spare batteries for all electronic devices, or a portable solar-panel recharger
	Fishing rod, tackle, flies or lures (optional)	
		Thermos (optional)
Backpack	1 backpack (smallest, lightest option appropriate for trip)	1 backpack (smallest, lightest option appropriate for trip)

FOOD

When planning the menu for your packrafting trip, it helps to think of the number of calories you need to sustain you through a long, hard day on the trail or river. Our size, gender, and activity level dictate how many calories we require each day. If sedentary, an average-size woman between the ages of 31 and 50 needs 1,800 calories per day. Sedentary men in that same age range need about 2,200 calories. Younger people typically need more calories; older, less. That number bumps up as you increase your

To help keep your pack weight down, weigh your food to ensure you bring enough to sustain you but not so much that you end up with leftovers.

activity level. Backpackers tend to burn twice as many calories as their sedentary peers, which means you need to make sure you are carrying enough food—around 4,000 calories per person per day—to perform well, feel good, and keep yourself safe.

The trick is to get the calories with as little weight as possible. You can find a lot of information online about lightweight food options. Here are a few tips to get you started.

Freeze-dried Meals

Probably the lightest, most efficient backcountry menu is to bring pre-packaged, freeze-dried meals for your entire trip. If you go this route, you may not even need to bring a bowl, as many freeze-dried meals are made by simply adding hot water to the pouch and letting the meal sit for a few minutes until it rehydrates.

Freeze-dried meals used to be pretty gross. The food often turned into a tasteless, mushy pile of glop when you added water. But times

Freeze-dried food is convenient and lightweight. You can add protein by adding packaged meat.

have changed, and now you can find some options that are varied and yummy, such as curried chicken and rice or pasta primavera for dinner and scrambled eggs and bacon for breakfast. Some of the best-known manufacturers of freeze-dried meals are AlpineAire, Backpacker's Pantry, Packit Gourmet, and Mountain House.

Combine these meals with instant coffee (Starbucks VIA is super lightweight and surprisingly good), hot chocolate, or tea and your cooking will involve nothing more than boiling water every day.

One problem with freeze-dried meals is their price, which varies from about $4 a serving to as much as $10. That can add up quickly if you plan to be out for a week eating only prepackaged meals. You may also want to do some taste tests before you go to make sure you like the flavor of the meals and to confirm the accuracy of the serving sizes. Sometimes a meal that is meant to serve two won't satisfy big eaters.

Home Drying

Drying your own fruit, vegetables, sauces, and meats is a great option if you have the time and motivation. There is a lot of information online on drying food, and Mike Clelland's *Ultralight Backpackin' Tips* has some

Your body will thank you if you keep your pack weight down by carrying lightweight food and gear.

simple recipes and ideas for ways to make your own backcountry meals at home. The end result will be not unlike prepackaged freeze-dried meals in that all you'll need to do is boil water to prepare your meal, but you'll save a lot of money, and you can tailor the amounts and flavor to your personal tastes.

Ziploc and Glad make plastic freezer bags that do not contain bisphenol A (BPA), so you can pour hot water directly into them to reconstitute your homemade freeze-dried meal. Simply cover the food by an inch or two of water, seal the bag, and let it sit wrapped up in a jacket or hat until the food is warm and soft.

If you do not like the idea of reconstituting your food in plastic bags, use a small pot that can be used both to heat water and as an eating bowl to streamline your kitchen needs. Again, it helps to wrap your pot in a coat while it sits to help keep your meal warm until it's ready to eat, or you can let it simmer over your stove if you have sufficient fuel.

From the Grocery Store

You can also just go shopping at the grocery store to pick out the food you need for your trip. Bulk food stores often have items like freeze-dried bean flakes or powdered hummus that make great lightweight food items. Instant rice in a bag, sauce packets like pesto or marinara, pasta, dried soup mixes—all these food items can be mixed and matched into a menu that is lightweight and often quite a bit cheaper than prepackaged freeze-dried meals. Be sure you re-bag your food so that you are carrying the amount you need without a lot of excess packaging. Freezer bags or two-ply plastic bags are strong and hold up better than thinner plastic bags. If you need spices for a particular meal, pour the desired amount into a small plastic bag (like the kind you use for buying bulk spices at the store) so you don't bring too much.

Packing Food

To make life as easy as possible, pack your meals for the day in a large freezer bag or a lightweight stuff sack. This helps you stay organized, especially if you have to store food in a bear canister, where it can be hard to find things when they are buried in the bottom. Mark the date for each package on the outside. Then all you need to do is pull out Monday's meals on Monday, leaving the rest of your week's supply packed up.

Developing Your Menu

Some lightweight backpackers like to cook on their own, even when they are traveling in a group. Others like to join forces and cook together, with different people taking turns for different days. If you go that route, which I personally prefer, you should know that it can be hard to plan a menu. Everyone has his or her particular likes and dislikes or special dietary needs. You can spread the challenge by having each member of your team assume responsibility for a day or two's worth of food. Or if you plan to have one person tackle the task, help him or her out by having your team answer a few questions before the trip, such as:

1. Do you have any food allergies?

2. Are you on a specific diet (gluten-free, vegetarian, vegan, etc.)?

3. List your favorite backcountry meal.

4. List your favorite backcountry snacks.

5. What foods do you refuse to eat?

6. What food could you eat nonstop for the entire trip?

7. Do you enjoy cooking in the field, or would you rather just boil water?

Breakfast and Dinner

Backpacking meals don't have to be all that different from the meals you cook at home. Your main constraints will be weight, appliances, time, heat source, and food preservation. Some people like to bring elaborate meals on their trips and are willing to carry the equipment needed to make those meals a success. Other people tend to go simple, preferring one-pot glop meals for the ease, speed, and lack of fuss or gear required to feed everyone. Since packrafters are already carrying roughly 15 pounds

Soylent

Soylent is a meal-replacement beverage available in both liquid and powder forms. According to its manufacturer, Soylent meets all nutritional requirements for an average adult. If you really want to go light, you might experiment with using Soylent powder for some of your meals.

of boating gear, most opt for the second option and go simple to keep their pack weight down.

Fast dinner options include pasta with pesto sauce, mac and cheese, or lentils and rice. You can up the calories by adding vacuum-packed meat such as tuna or chicken to give you some protein and extra calories for when you are working hard. Easy breakfasts can be granola and dried milk, instant oatmeal, or polenta and cheese.

Lunch

There's a saying among backpackers that lunch starts when breakfast ends and ends when dinner begins. Basically you will want to snack all day long to maintain your energy levels during exertion. It's nice to have something that actually resembles a meal—cheese and crackers and summer sausage, for example—that you can supplement with snacks like cracker mix, mixed nuts, gorp, dried fruit, or energy bars.

Look for breads and crackers that aren't too bulky. Pita bread and tortillas are good because they pack easily and can withstand a little compression. Dense crackers with lots of seeds also tend to stand up to packing well and provide some protein in addition to carbohydrates.

Smoked meats, jerky, and fish or chicken in foil packets are good sources of protein, although they are a little heavy, so use them sparingly. Cheese is packed with calories, protein, and fat and can also be a good source of fuel, particularly when temperatures are cold and the weather is damp. Harder cheeses tend to keep better than soft cheeses, but even hard cheese can get a little oily and soft if the temperatures are hot during

Energy Bars

Most grocery stores now have an entire aisle dedicated to energy bars. If you believe the hype, energy bars are the new miracle food. They can give you instant energy, lots of protein, extra minerals, fiber, and vitamins. They can help you lose weight or power you through an ultra run with energy to spare. You name it, you can find it in a bar. The question is, how much of this is marketing hype and how much of it is true? Energy bars have some distinctive advantages. They are portable, packed with calories, and have a long shelf life, which makes them a convenient backpacking food. Balance those things against some of the negatives, however, and the answer is more ambiguous. Many energy bars are expensive and can be high in sugar, sodium, and preservatives. Sometimes a single bar is meant to be two servings, and the number of calories in even one serving can be quite high. Read the label. The best energy bars have a balance of complex and simple carbohydrates so that they don't just give you a sugar rush before a subsequent crash.

your hike. You can help minimize that by packing your cheese deep inside your backpack, where it is insulated from the heat of the sun. Even if the cheese gets a little soft, it is still fine to eat. Some people like to bring individually wrapped, single-serving chunks of cheese that you can find in the deli section of your grocery store. These can help you plan ahead and control serving sizes.

STOVES

Think about the type of cooking you intend to do as you make your decision about the type of stove to carry. If you are simply boiling water on a summer packrafting trip with a friend, a homemade alcohol stove (find directions for making your own online) is a good way to go. But alcohol stoves are not great if your group is larger than two and if you want to control the intensity of your heat source. Basically alcohol stoves have two settings: on and off.

Mixed-fuel cartridge stoves provide an instant flame with variable intensity and are small (although the cartridges themselves are rather

For groups of two preparing simple meals that only require boiling water, alcohol stoves are light and cheap.

bulky). White gas stoves are the heaviest option available, but they work well in cold temperatures (below freezing) and are easy to repair in the field. They are also the easiest to bake on if you get ambitious in your meal planning and are ideal for larger groups where meals take longer to prepare.

Lots of packrafters like to cook on fires. Cooking on fires means you only have to carry a lighter, matches, and maybe some kind of fire starter,

If you plan to cook on campfires in places without a lot of trees and deadfall, it's a good idea to collect driftwood during the day to use in camp.

so it's the lightest option out there. Before going this route, make sure your trip is in an area that allows fires and has plenty of downed wood available to burn. Fires also work best if you don't anticipate camping in the rain for the duration of your expedition. Not that you can't make a fire when it's damp out, but it is certainly more time-consuming than simply lighting a stove, and it can be a bummer to sit in the rain trying to light a fire when your stomach is growling.

To keep your pots from getting black and dirty, burn the creosote and carbon off them in the fire after you are done cooking. You can also carry a lightweight stuff sack to keep your pot separate from the other items inside your backpack.

Another lightweight option is a twiggy stove that burns small pieces of wood in a contained space to heat your food. Twiggy stoves are a little slower and dirtier than alcohol stoves, but you don't have to carry any fuel to use one. Make sure to check on fire regulations before deciding to go this route. You'll be in trouble if there's a fire ban and all you have is a twiggy stove.

Stove Choices

Alcohol stoves

- Good for 1–2 people
- Lightweight, cheap
- Best for boiling water; no way to moderate heat output

Mixed-fuel cartridge stoves

- Easy to use; do not require priming
- Heat output can be controlled to allow simmering
- Cartridges can be bulky and on a long trip will add weight and take up space
- Do not work well in temperatures below freezing

White gas stoves

- Heavy, but good for groups of 4 or more
- Easy to repair in the field
- Heat output adjustable, allows simmering, boiling, baking
- Work well in cold temperatures

Fires or twiggy stoves

- Need to be in an area that allows fires and has plenty of firewood
- Lightweight
- Can be time-consuming and challenging to light in wet conditions
- Blackens pots, so good idea to carry a stuff sack for keeping pots away from gear

KITCHEN NEEDS

The most lightweight option out there is to go with food you don't need to cook at all. This kind of food might not be lighter than a freeze-dried meal, but you won't need to carry a stove, fuel, pots, and utensils. A no-cook menu includes preserved meats, cheese, energy bars, bread, crackers, nuts, dried fruit, and trail mix. Most backpackers find that this kind of grazing food loses its allure rather quickly on an extended trip. There's something nice about a hot meal at the end of a long day that is appealing to most of us, especially if the weather is less than perfect. But if you are out for a quick trip, skipping hot meals can lessen the weight in your pack.

Assuming you plan to cook, the lightest kitchen you can carry will include nothing more than a small pot that can double as a bowl or cup, a lightweight stove, and a spoon that can be used for eating or stirring.

If you want to be a bit more elaborate, you can carry a bigger pot that allows you to cook for more than one person at a time. You may also want to include a small frying pan and a spatula for frying or baking. These are definitely luxury items, but when you are on an extended expedition, they can provide welcome variety to your food. Remove all plastic parts from your frying pan so that you can use it in a fire or to bake without worrying about melting the handle off.

It's a good idea to bring a container for transporting water. Most national forests and parks require that you make camp at least 200 feet from water sources, so to avoid constant trips back and forth, carry something like a 3-liter MSR Dromedary or a plastic collapsible water jug for storing water.

WATER TREATMENT

To be on the safe side, especially in areas with a lot of backcountry visitors, wildlife, or livestock, it's best to treat your water. Anyone who has suffered from giardiasis knows that the effects of drinking contaminated water are pretty miserable.

There are lots of water treatment options out there. The simplest is to heat your water. Contrary to popular belief, you don't have to boil water for 5 minutes to make it safe. In fact, you don't even have to boil it at all. Most disease-causing organisms are killed or rendered harmless at temperatures well below the boiling point of 212°F. Fish eyes—or the point when you see small bubbles along the sides and bottom of your pot—is hot enough to kill the things that will make you sick.

You can also use chemicals such as iodine tablets, liquid chlorine dioxide (Aquamira), or a filter to purify your water.

In clear water, a handheld ultraviolet light can be used to purify your water in 90 seconds or less.

In the past few years, people have begun using ultraviolet light to cleanse their water. SteriPEN is the leading manufacturer of these hand-held devices that purify water in 90 seconds or less without any added taste from chemicals. The downside to SteriPENs is that they require batteries or a charge to operate, are heavier than a little bottle of iodine tablets, and do not work in murky water.

Silty Water

If you travel on glacial rivers or in the desert, your primary water sources may be full of silt. SteriPENs and filters do not work in silty water, and most of us have a pretty hard time drinking water that looks like chocolate milk anyway. Sometimes you can find clear water flowing in tributaries to the main river channel. Other times you'll need to collect water and let it sit for a couple of hours to let the silt settle out. If you are in a hurry, try pouring the silty water through a bandana into a pot. The bandana will help filter out a lot of the suspended particles in the water. You will still need to treat the water to make it potable.

Silty water can be hard to purify and less than appealing to drink. You can sometimes find clear water in side streams. If you have no choice, filter the water through a bandana to help remove the silt.

APPENDIX A: SAMPLE FIRST-AID KIT

YOUR FIRST-AID KIT WILL BE DETERMINED IN PART BY THE LENGTH OF your trip, the number of participants, and the remoteness of your destination. The following list can be tailored to meet your needs.

Wound Care
- ☐ 2–4 packages of sterile gauze pads of various sizes (packages generally contain two pads)
- ☐ 2–4 non-adherent sterile dressings, such as Tegaderm patches
- ☐ Fabric bandages of various sizes
- ☐ 1 roll 1-inch athletic tape
- ☐ Moleskin or blister pads
- ☐ 1 needle-nose syringe
- ☐ 3 alcohol swab packets
- ☐ 4 triple-antibiotic ointment packets
- ☐ 1 packet of wound-closure strips (Steri-Strips)
- ☐ 4–5 antiseptic towelettes
- ☐ Nitrile gloves (1–2 pairs)
- ☐ Skin-Tac topical adhesive (tincture of benzoin)

Insect Bites
- ☐ Anti-itch cream, such as hydrocortisone or After Bite Itch Eraser

Sprains or Strains
- ☐ 1 2-inch elastic bandage with Velcro closure (Ace bandage)
- ☐ 1 roll self-adhering vet tape, such as Dura-Tech Vet Flex

Miscellaneous
- ☐ 1 pair tweezers
- ☐ Scissors
- ☐ 1 breathing barrier or pocket mask
- ☐ Pencil and patient assessment form

APPENDIX B: SAMPLE NOLS WILDERNESS MEDICINE INSTITUTE PATIENT ASSESSMENT FORM

SOAP NOTES

SOAP NOTES ARE A COMMONLY USED FORMAT FOR RECORDING MEDICAL information in emergency situations. A SOAP note includes:

- Subjective information
- Objective information
- An Assessment
- A Plan

SOAP notes are useful for first aiders as a guide for organizing their actions and for reporting information to more qualified help.

Subjective information is the stuff your patient tells you, such as his name and his version of events. It includes the patient's age, history of the illness or injury, and the chief complaint (including a description of the associated symptoms).

Objective information is measurable and includes vital signs, results from the head-to-toe exam, and the SAMPLE history (Signs and symptoms, Allergies, Medications, Past medical history, Last intake and outtake, Events leading up to present situation).

The **assessment** is your best guess at what is going on. You may not have any medical training, but you've watched enough television over the years to guess that the 50-year-old man in your party who is describing radiating pain in his chest may be having some kind of heart problem and needs immediate medical attention. Likewise, you can guess from the

Wilderness First Responder SOAP Note

Name _____ **Date** _____

Location _____

Subjective/Summary/Story *(age, sex, chief complaint, OPQRST, MOI/HPI).*
_____
_____

Objective/Observations/Findings *(Describe position found. Describe injuries).*
_____
_____

Patient Exam _____
_____
_____

Vital Signs

Time			
LOR			
HR			
RR			
SCTM			
BP			
Pupils			
Temp			

History

Symptoms_____

Allergies_____

Medications_____

Pertinent Medical History_____

Last Intake/Output_____

Events recent _____

Assessment *(List Problems)* _____
_____
_____

Plan *(Plan for each problem)*_____
_____

Anticipated problems _____
_____

SOAP notes, such as this one from NOLS, can be easily searched and printed off the Internet. NOLS

fact that your partner's ankle is the size of a grapefruit and she said she twisted it stepping off a boulder that she has likely sprained or broken the affected joint.

No doctor expects you to be able to diagnose medical problems, but writing down your best guess based on your understanding of the signs and symptoms you've recorded helps the doctor understand where you were coming from. It also helps you determine the urgency of your treatment plan.

There are certain conditions for which you can do very little in the field, such as head, neck, and back injuries; chest injuries; or serious illness. If you suspect any of these problems after conducting your patient exam, you should try to make your patient as comfortable as possible and seek immediate help, whether that means calling out on a satellite phone or radio, running to a road, flagging down another party, or hitting the emergency button on a personal locator beacon.

The **plan** includes everything that happens next. This includes immediate steps—splinting the fractured leg or cleaning the wound—as well as long-term care, such as how you intend to make your patient comfortable until the injury heals or you can get him or her to a hospital. Can your patient stay with you in the wilderness, or does he have to see a doctor? If your patient needs medical attention, can she walk out of the wilderness or are you going to need assistance? What kind of assistance is available? These kinds of questions all need to be addressed in your plan.

APPENDIX C: SAMPLE DRUG KIT

- Acetaminophen (500 mg tablets)
- Ibuprofen (200 mg tablets)
- Antihistamine (diphenhydramine or Benadryl)
- Diamode or other antidiarrheal medication
- Antacid

Prescription Meds

For extended trips to remote locations, talk to your doctor about securing the following medications for emergencies:

- Pain-relief medications such as Vicodin, Tylenol 2, or Stadol NS
- Antibiotics for bacterial infections (wound, gastrointestinal, sinus, eye, ear, or respiratory)
- Epinephrine in the form of an EpiPen or Ana-Kit to treat severe allergic reactions

If you have a medical condition that requires special medications or you are allergic to bee stings or other allergens and carry epinephrine, make sure your teammates are aware of your situation. Make a list of important information about your condition and the medications you use to treat it, and keep that list in your med kit in case of an emergency where you cannot explain your needs to a caregiver.

Be sure to include the following information:

- Name of the drug (both generic and proprietary)
- Dose, including the amount and frequency

- Uses and indications of why and when to take the drug
- Contraindications or reasons not to take the drug
- Possible side effects or adverse reactions
- Things not to mix with the drug (e.g., alcohol)
- Description of the medication (size, color, shape) in case pills get mixed up

APPENDIX D: SAMPLE GROUP REPAIR KIT (NON-BOATING)

- Duct tape or Tyvek tape (wrap spare duct tape around a trekking pole or water bottle rather than carry a full roll in your kit)
- Multi-tool with scissors
- Needle and dental floss
- Spare parts for stove
- Nylon utility cord (50 feet)
- Tent pole repair sleeve
- Inflatable mattress repair kit
- Spare batteries and bulbs for headlamps
- Spare hip belt buckle and cord locks
- Seam Grip (can be used for many repairs, from sealing boot soles to patching tents)

INDEX

bracing, 86–91
and capsizing, 153–54, *155*
choosing objective, 141, 143, 144
clothing for, 31–43
communicating while, 124–30
current state of, 5, 7
draw stroke, 84–86
eddy turns, 93–99
and environmental regulations, 175–81
equipment for, 8, *9, 10*
ferrying, 91–93
foot entrapment, 156
forward stroke, 74–78
mental preparation for, 144–47
open-boat paddling, 132, 134
origins of, 1–5
paddle signals, 128–30
paddling position, 130–32, 134
pirouette (spin), 99
practicing, 99
in rapids, 135–41
reading currents, 100–102
rescuing a swimmer, 155–60
risk in, 147–50, 151–53
sweep stroke, 79–84
teamwork and rescues, 162–63
whitewater terms, 133
See also clothing; first aid; gear; packrafts; rivers; trips, planning
Packrafting! (Dial), 3, 54, 203
packrafts, 5, 6
attaching load to, 53–59
cargo storage on, 19–20
cleaning and drying, 61–62
costs of, 8
deflating and packing up, 61
D-rings and tie-downs on, 195–96
early, 1–4
getting in and out of, 59–60, 65–69
grab line, 23

holding onto if overboard, 153–54, *155*
inflating, 21, *22,* 47–53
maneuvering rapids and holes, 135–41
paddles for, 24–25
paddling position and technique, 63–65, 69–70
pinned, 160–62
repairing, 185–95
rolling, 152
seats of, 21–22, 52–53
self-bailing or spray deck, 14, 15
stern lines on, 20, *21*
styles of, 10–14
thigh straps on, 15–16, 17, 18, 87, 197–99
and waves, 134–35
See also packrafting; specific raft brands
paddles, 24–25, 130–32
"catching a crab," 86
hand position on, 70–74
and low or high braces, 88–91
repairing, 194–95
signals with, 128–30
See also packrafts
paddling suits, 32–33, 39
personal flotation devices (PFDs), 25–29
pogies, 40, 41, *42*

R
rapids. *See* rivers
repair kits, 46, 187, 246
rescue vests, 29
See also personal flotation devices (PFDs)
river knives, 44
river running. *See* packrafting
rivers
bends and channels in, 102–3

ABOUT THE AUTHOR

Molly Absolon has written ten titles for the *Backpacker* Magazine Outdoor Skills Series (Falcon). She is also the author of *Basic Illustrated Winter Camping* and *Basic Illustrated Alpine Ski Touring*. Molly spent years working as an outdoor educator for the National Outdoor Leadership School, and her experience teaching technical skills to beginners translates on the page into instructions that are easy to read and follow. Molly is a packrafter who has found that her 5-pound boat has transformed the way she looks at a map and explores the backcountry. She lives in Victor, Idaho, with her husband and daughter.

RAVITZ